THE
SECRETS
OF WEALTH

Discover the financial principles
responsible for every fortune ever made.

Learn how *you too* can apply these principles
step-by-step, to create your own fortune.

PARVIZ FIROUZGAR

i

The Secrets of Wealth

by

Parviz Firouzgar

Cover Design by Melodye Hunter
Copyright © 2015 by Parviz Firouzgar.
Interior Design by Zonoiko Arafat

ISBN: 978-0-9964269-8-5

Crescendo Publishing, LLC
300 Carlsbad Village Drive
Ste. 108A, #443
Carlsbad, California 92008-2999

www.CrescendoPublishing.com
GetPublished@CrescendoPublishing.com

Crescendo

A Message from the Author

Download a complimentary BONUS chapter from my next book, *"20/20 Hindsight – Additional Lessons"* here:

http://www.parvizfirouzgar.com/

What People Are Saying About "The Secrets of Wealth"

"I am just speechless. As I was reading the first couple chapters I just couldn't stop thinking, "Why the heck is this not being taught in schools?" In this smart, insightful and fascinating book, Parviz gives you exactly how anyone can grow their money by using universal laws. No matter if you are earning a meager salary or are making millions, this book is a step-by-step guide as to how to multiply what you have and achieve financial freedom."

~Santiago Restrepo
Entrepreneur

"The Secrets of Wealth truly delivers on its promise. I found it staggeringly pertinent and incredibly practical for anybody who has begun on their quest for a higher quality of life. Truly, if you were searching for a treasure map and ran across this book, you would have found one. I highly recommend that you read this book, and then read it again and again. Your success is practically guaranteed. I absolutely loved it and gathered more gems from these pages than any other I've ever read before!"

~Vicky Prince
Success Coach

"A needed breath of fresh air amidst the collection of personal finance books. Parviz Firouzgar has assembled a priceless collection of immediately actionable strategies proven to work in growing your wealth and success. I have personally benefitted from these approaches in my own life and trust that readers will find the same."

~Nick Stoianov, Ph.D
Developers Lead, EBay Inc.

"Parviz Firouzgar is not just a seeker; he's a finder. He has found little-known secrets of wealth which, when combined with the usual methods, may well compound the creation of wealth to higher and higher levels. This book is like a mentor-in-print about wealth creation. As the author admits, this is not original thinking but time-proven methods, in some cases dating back thousands of years. These principles and secrets are about abundance in agreement with the laws of nature, not merely the thoughts of man."

~Tom Justin
Author, *How To Take No For An Answer and Still Succeed*

"The Secrets of Wealth is a MUST read for anyone that wants to change their life or help someone else change theirs! This is a modern-day Science of Getting Rich. It's not a one-time read, it's an everyday read!"

~Dave Phillipson
Author & Regional Director, CEO Space

"Parviz Firouzgar has written a great follow up to his previous book 20/20 Hindsight. His new book *The Secrets of Wealth* is also destined to become a bestseller as it uses insights from such great minds as Archimedes and then lays out their financial principles in an easy to understand step-by-step plan. Readers can feel confident that they too can acquire great wealth if they apply the principles explained in this book."

~Stephen Kent
Entrepreneur

"There is so much I can say about Parviz Firouzgar's book and still not do it justice. There are so many wealth-building books published today, but none of them give you the mentoring navigation like *The Secrets of Wealth*. It provides specific details, direct examples and most importantly, this WORKS!"

~B. Smith
Fmr. Federal Financial Institutions Regulator

"Once again Parviz has raised the bar on wealth and business planning literary works. *The Secrets of Wealth* helps to provide anyone who wants to improve their financial world a real life, down to earth perspective that will serve to de-mystify the path to true and enduring financial prosperity."

~Dustin I. Nichols Esq.
The Law Office of Dustin I. Nichols, A PC

"Wow! This book has given me a whole new look at managing my financials and inspired me with numerous truths that can make my money work for me. Where the book 'The Richest Man in Babylon' leaves off, Parviz has picked up and continues with more wealth creating techniques. He illustrates why the average individual hasn't reached or achieved their full potential, what mistakes they make and how wealth and success have eluded them. Parviz even breaks down the information into simple steps that anyone who reads this scholastic manuscript may start implementing right away to gain wealth. There is so much great information in *The Secrets of Wealth* that I find myself going back and reading it over and over again."

~Raul J. Casiano Rosado
Mortgage Broker

"*The Secrets to Wealth* is the ultimate template for success. It's a must-read and must-follow for anyone with any means that wants to be, and more importantly feel, rich."

~Raymond F. Olmo, CEP®, RFC®
Managing Director, Trust-CFO

Dedication

I dedicate this book to Man's Work:

Man's work is a monument to himself.
At its unveiling he sees the marks
of his striving as the Master Sculptor.
He carves away the marble piece
to let come forth the form of his work.
His work includes himself:
The work itself being an activity
of the ever widening environment
of his world of thought.
In time it is polished and engraved
with his approving word, "Well Done."

–Nita Yore Kelsey

Table of Contents

"How to become a millionaire...
first, get a million dollars."
–Steve Martin

Introduction

Have you ever wondered how the rich got to be rich? What do they know that you don't? If you knew their secrets, could you become rich also?

For centuries, wealth has been created by individuals armed with the right knowledge, knowledge that is not widely known. This book is about that knowledge.

In most methods of wealth creation, there are underlying common ingredients, financial principles that naturally multiply money. *The Secrets of Wealth* explores these common ingredients and compiles them to show you how money accumulates and how fortunes can be made. The principles described in this text have universal applications, and they are timeless.

The Secrets of Wealth also contains a how-to guide. It is presented as a sequential to-do list and shows you how you can apply the financial principles described in this text. It offers you a means to escape the financial quagmire that imprisons most people, and it will show you how to create financial security for the rest of your life.

The Secrets of Wealth will provide you with the tools necessary to achieve financial independence. The methods contained in the following pages will work for anyone from almost any starting point, even from a very modest income. They can work in present-day America and remain relevant anywhere and anytime in the future. Step-by-step instructions will guide you from a fixed income to financial prosperity. In fact, this book will empower you to take the concept of creating personal wealth from mystery to mastery.

The secrets referenced in the title of this text are a series of truths that have been known for many generations. In fact, some of the principles you will discover in the following pages have been available to us for over five thousand years. However, only a few individuals have known where to find them. Fewer still have had the wisdom to understand their effectiveness. Before one can realize the financial potential these principles contain, they must first be recognized and then thoroughly understood. Unfortunately, no one has been there to point them out to us, much less to explain their hidden power. That is about to change.

Revealed to you will be a series of absolute truths that govern the behavior of money and the accumulation of wealth. They are the laws of fiscal health and the multiplication of money. At first these principles may fool you. You may think they are too simple to be effective. Actually, they are effective because of their simplicity. Winston Churchill said, "All great things are simple." He was right.

Some of the universal principles of wealth outlined in this text were first found inscribed on ancient clay tablets in the ruins of Babylon, where they had been used by the elite. In fact, these principles were responsible for the elite in the first place. Relatively speaking, Babylon was one of the most prosperous cities that ever existed. It had a highly developed monetary system with banks and credit that was far ahead of its time.

It is those same principles that are responsible for most wealthy individuals in the world today. The problem is that most middle-income people do not have access to the wisdom of the wealthy.

How often have we heard, "Take away every penny owned by a wealthy individual, and he will earn it all back." This is a true statement, and it tells us that there has to be a method. Once you learn the art of wealth creation, you will be able to duplicate it even if all your money is suddenly lost. In fact, once you learn these techniques, even if you do lose everything, your second time around will be easier and faster.

Millionaires often say, "The first million dollars was the most difficult. After the first," they reveal, "the others come easily." Why? Because these individuals now possess knowledge they did not have prior to accumulating their first million dollars. Their second million was not a result of the first. It does not take money to make money as is so often claimed by those who are broke. What the nouveau riche learn is that there are similarities to all methods of accumulating wealth, and these methods can be applied virtually anywhere.

It is these common ingredients that make up the principles we shall explore. They are very simple to understand, not difficult to implement, and they can work for you too. Furthermore, when you grasp how the ensuing principles apply to all aspects of your life, not just financial, then you can benefit from the information in additional ways that will become increasingly clear to you later.

Let's talk about money.

This book is about making money, not about becoming successful. There is a difference. Success is not about money; it is about fulfillment. It is about doing what you love and making a living doing it. When you follow your passion and become successful, the money will automatically follow. I have written and lectured extensively about success, and this book will contain some of that information also. However, I wrote this book primarily to share financial principles with you that have to do with only one thing—multiplying your money.

One of the reasons I have chosen to share this inside information with you is that the more wealth that is created, the more it continues to multiply for everyone. In other words, we all benefit from each other's contribution to creating more wealth. If you make a million dollars in your own business, chances are you are providing several jobs to your fellow man. If you make your fortune in the stock market, you'll probably go out and spend a substantial portion of it, benefiting the merchants who receive your patronage. In at least a dozen ways, every extra dollar you earn benefits our economy and therefore all of us. Whether you call it trickledown economics or sharing the wealth, it works for everyone. Money is not the root of all evil; it is the root of all civilization.

The principles of wealth have been around for several millennia, yet they have remained inaccessible to most of us. Ultimately it is your right to have access to this information because it is everyone's divine right to seek wealth and freedom. Furthermore, our pursuit of happiness is made substantially easier if we are prosperous.

Democracies are all about the freedom to choose. But freedom is not free. Because wealth buys freedom—*the freedom to choose alternatives not available to those without it*—it follows that we should seek wealth if we want to exercise our freedom to the fullest. Freedom of choice and freedom of wealth are inseparable.

Wealth is the pursuit and achievement of happiness as made possible, or at least easier, by the accumulation of money. True wealth is to be able to spend your life your way.

The result is personal freedom.

The preceding statements should not be read to support the cliché that money will make you happy. There are countless tales of the rich and famous who are as miserable as can be, while their money grants them neither joy nor freedom. Their narcissistic egos and obsessive fears of losing their wealth eliminate any joy that should have been the fruit of their achievements. It does imply that material wealth is a powerful vehicle that can aid you in fulfilling your dreams and goals.

Benjamin Franklin wrote, "Wealth is not his that has it, but his that enjoys it." Nonetheless, the old axiom, "Money cannot make you happy, but it does allow you to choose the kind of misery you enjoy most," is as true as ever.

Wealth is a means to an end rather than an end in itself. Actually, wealth is a means to better ends, such as a better future. It follows that society could justifiably condemn those who devote their whole lives to making and hoarding money. I'm referring to those individuals who justify any means that can advance the pursuit of riches for its own sake. The individual who loves money more than what it can accomplish demonstrates a self-indulgent, misguided, and highly destructive affection for our greenback.

Because we live in a material world, it is up to us to use or deny the tools made available to us. Among these tools, money is neutral, neither good nor bad. We decide whether to use it for constructive or for destructive purposes. It has been said that money makes a bad man worse and a good man better. In fact, once you make your first fortune, when the world sees how you use your wealth, you and those around you will find out who you really are. For better or for worse, there will be no hiding it.

Because the choice is not easy, with temptation lurking at every corner, this is a far greater responsibility than most realize. If we use money for destructive purposes, what we will accumulate is not true wealth. We will not be enriched by such wealth—materially, spiritually, or otherwise. True wealth is never measured in solely monetary terms. It has been said that true wealth is that which is left after the money is gone.

Finally, the key to the argument in favor of sharing this wealth-making information with you is in assisting you in your ability to be generous.

It is in the generosity of the middle class and the affluent that the meek find hope. It is a blessing not only to the unfortunate in need but also to those who find satisfaction in helping those who need help. Many individuals want to be generous for its own sake but are denied this basic source of joy because of their own need. Wealth benefits us all, and as such, poverty is the greatest injustice you can perpetrate upon yourself or your fellow man.

Contrary to popular belief, it is our entrepreneurial upper class that creates jobs for the less fortunate, and it is our upper class that donates the majority of funds to the needy. If we were to strip away the upper-income portion of our society, the result would be devastating. First and foremost, our economy would collapse as the largest source of employment would be removed from our infrastructure. Removed also would be the pool of capital that enables most entrepreneurs and small firms to establish themselves as contributing parts of society.

It is wealthy individuals who fund most new ventures, not banks or venture-capital firms. It is also the thousands of small to medium-sized firms that provide the majority of jobs in all sectors of the economy. There are currently only about 2,000 corporations in America with over 5,000 employees, but there are over a half million companies with twenty to ninety-nine employees, and almost 100,000 companies with 100–499 employees. Do the math.

Wealth enables our potential to be generous. America has always been the most charitable country in the world. No other country even comes close. This is not a coincidence.

It is wealthy individuals who provide most of the financial support for hundreds of charitable organizations worldwide, from the Red Cross and American Cancer Society to Amnesty International and Mothers Against Drunk Driving. In 2013 total charitable donations reached a record $335 billion. That's astounding! Whether for humanitarian reasons or for tax deductions, the upper-income portion of our society provides the majority of support for these organizations.

"No one would have remembered the Good Samaritan if he'd only had good intentions. He had money as well."

–Margaret Thatcher

It should be noted that most current savings reserves in America come almost entirely from the wealthy. This is not enough. The middle class has to participate also. The base of our savings must be dramatically increased for the long-term well-being of our nation. This can be done only by elevating the lower and middle classes to a higher level of financial security.

Because our government provides the worst role model of all, it is now up to us to help ourselves. In fact, it is our duty to do so. Each of us is a wheel in the giant machine we call the national economy. Therefore, each of us is responsible for our fair share in keeping this machine running so that we may all benefit. Right now it is in desperate need of a tune-up, and there are only two ways to accomplish this.

First, we could fire, or at least not re-elect, the misfits we have elected to office who are responsible for our hijacked political system, staggering debt, and out-of-control spending. Unfortunately it seems that we, as a nation, repeatedly reject making any significant changes to our congressional makeup as we consistently re-elect 98 percent of all incumbents.

The last resort amounts to us learning what it takes to become significant enough economically — as individuals

— by means of creating wealth, to positively impact America's economy. That is what this book is all about, and that is one of the reasons I am sharing this information with you.

America is at a critical juncture. When we talk about an $18 trillion national debt, rising unemployment, the threat of inflation, a banking crisis, or a host of other economic calamities, we are dealing with indicators that make interesting news but are abstract to the average working American. Most people cannot relate to a trillion dollars or even to a banking crisis as the effects of such crises on our lives are often indirect.

Without the aforementioned improvements that are critical to our future prosperity, middle-income families may be forced to take additional drastic measures to maintain their standard of living. In the past there has always been some room for tightening our belts. But that is no longer the case.

During the recession of the Carter administration, what major social change took place, allowing individuals to cope with runaway price increases? Many people began to share their living quarters to save money. The concept of roommates became commonplace for the first time outside the college environment.

Later in the same decade we needed more steps to keep up. The solution became dual-income households. Conveniently, this coincided with the feminist movement, so the need became cleverly disguised as women's demand for equality.

Now what is happening? If you ask many middle-class citizens, they'll tell you they are working two jobs or at least considering a second source of income. This assumes that they can even find employment as our current true unemployment rate is closer to 23 percent, not the 6 or 7 percent the government would like you to believe.

So now that we have our middle-class citizens who cannot afford to live alone, where wives also have to work to make ends meet, and where many have to work more than one job, what comes next? Will we have to sacrifice our children's college funds or our retirement nest eggs? Scarce as they may be already, and with job security being a thing of the past, we're in trouble.

Even if society invents another adjustment to our style of living that enables us to temporarily keep pace, there can be only one long-term solution. Our standard of living has to be high enough so that on a personal level, our government's repeated economic failures are paid for with our excess cash, not the money we need to cover our bills. Excess cash means savings—lots of savings. We will still experience the same anger every time we have to bail out Uncle Sam's ineptitude, but at least our lives will not be turned upside down every time it happens. This is the advantage of being wealthy.

Consider this: During the recession of 2008, over two million jobs were lost. Unemployment in some sectors of the country surpassed 25 percent. However, for people previously earning more than $100,000 per year, unemployment was closer to 1 percent. The lesson is twofold. One, if your income is high enough, then you probably have adequate savings to weather the next storm. But more importantly, high-income earners have learned skills that enable them to continue earning in almost any economic environment. Successful entrepreneurs are highest on that list. They have learned transferrable skills that can be utilized in whatever industry is currently profitable. Essentially, successful entrepreneurs have learned how to create their own jobs regardless of economic climate.

It is my opinion that any serious prosperity plan must also take into consideration your ideology toward wealth. Your core belief system predisposes your ability to succeed. Individuals with an antagonistic mindset toward wealth will have to change their orientation before they can become financially successful. For example, if you believe that all wealth is the result of dishonest activity, then you carry with you a mental block that will keep you from becoming financially successful. That's a mathematical certainty.

Society's disposition toward financial prosperity must also be considered as it affects our views and the environment we work in. It will therefore also impact our ability to fulfill our financial goals. The impact is always profoundly in favor of, or in opposition to, free enterprise and wealth accumulation. The unfortunate truth is that many people, including those in government, frown upon wealth. That is, *our* wealth. Their wealth is quite acceptable to them.

As mentioned previously, wealth undoubtedly does bring with it a certain amount of temptation. There are those individuals who have succumbed to excessive greed and misuse of that which they have earned. Their morals and values have been all but forgotten. Maybe some people go down this road because of the inaccurate perceptions they have been taught as they grew up.

Society has taught us to feel guilty if we have too much money. Historically, the lower and middle classes have been taught to equate wealth with evil, probably because 90 percent of wealthy individuals are honest, hardworking people who therefore never make the news. It is those that abuse their wealth, the other 10 percent, like Bernie Madoff, that we hear about. Even the Bible states that it is harder for a rich man to enter the kingdom of heaven than it is for a camel to pass through the eye of a needle. Furthermore, the Bible preaches, "It is the meek who shall inherit the Earth." If we fail to look past the symbolism in these quotes, is it any wonder that we grow up with skewed perceptions toward the rich? Besides, the only thing the meek shall inherit is our national debt.

Our skewed perception toward wealthy people, combined with the misguided efforts of Congress to solve our fiscal problems, have led to a "soak the rich" movement. This philosophy was superbly illustrated by the luxury tax imposed during the '90s, whereby any high-ticket item costing over a certain amount ($30,000 on cars) was assessed a 10 percent value-added tax on the amount over $30,000. At the time it was supposedly enacted to help balance the federal budget.

The problem was that it was taking in far less than it was costing. It actually cost five dollars for every dollar it brought in. Here we finally had the proof that raising taxes does not necessarily raise revenues. Rather than allow the government to rob them, able buyers simply kept their wallets in their pockets. The rich did not get rich by being stupid. Wouldn't you do the same if you were considering buying a million-dollar yacht only to find that you would have to pay an additional $97,000 just to pay for the government's continued incompetence and staggering bureaucracy?

This tax resulted in idling thousands of workers who made and sold luxury items. The American boat industry was almost destroyed as a result of this misguided strategy, and our ability to compete overseas was crippled. Yacht sales fell 85 percent in the first six months of 1991, and 19,000 workers were scheduled to be laid off. The effect on suppliers to the boat industry was incalculable, and the resulting outlays for unemployment insurance made this tax a national calamity. As you may recall, the tax has been repealed, but the damage was done, and I guarantee no lessons were learned.

The same problems exist with income taxes. We do not need higher taxes. We need more efficient taxation, especially when taxes are targeted solely at the rich. High taxes stifle investment and economic growth.

To paraphrase Alan Greenspan, former chairman of the Federal Reserve, "All taxes have a negative economic impact. Taxes should be used to encourage values that are of greater benefit than the negative economic impact they impose." That is, beyond a level of equilibrium, taxes do not raise more revenues because the negative economic impact is greater than the money raised.

Arthur Laffer proved this with his Laffer curve. It showed the relationship between levels of taxation and the actual revenues they produce. When taxes are increased beyond a certain level, they become counterproductive. The money raised will not meet expectations because the economic consequences of excessive tax increases actually cause a decrease in total collections. It is therefore the responsibility of government to seek a level of equilibrium where collections are at an acceptable level and the economy does not suffer as a result.

If we can ever get the government to stop throwing our money away, we may even want to consider lowering income taxes for those individuals making a real contribution to society—the wealthy. A regressive tax would instantly motivate people to work harder in order to move into higher income brackets. The percentage of tax they would pay on their income would diminish, but total tax collections would increase without burdening those who are truly victims of undeserved hardship.

The rationale is the following: if free enterprise has created a very efficient system whereby businesses stimulate more trade through volume discounts on larger orders, why would a similar rationale applied to taxation not work to increase tax receipts?

Admittedly, the preceding scenarios are simplistic, and the regressive tax is politically impossible to enact (it's much too logical for Congress), but it does get us thinking in the right direction. I believe that Winston Churchill showed remarkable insight into the futility of draining the rich when he said, "You don't make the poor richer by making the rich poorer." However, when it comes to wealthy individuals, I do want to make a distinction.

There is a huge difference between most millionaires and the majority of billionaires. This profound difference has been confirmed by studies and analysis. Millionaires, with some exceptions, are mostly honest, hardworking individuals who deserve every dollar they have earned. As already mentioned, they are also the most important contributors to our economy, charities, and tax collections. Billionaires, on the other hand, are a completely different breed of people. Most of them consider themselves to be anointed into their position of obscene wealth and influence with a divinely inspired purpose to rule over us and make themselves richer by any means possible.

Many billionaires are or have become sociopaths. That is, they have little or no conscience and will do anything to further their wealth, power, cause, and agenda. These people are clearly not whom I refer to when I speak of wealthy individuals. I refer to millionaires, not billionaires, because billionaires are the root of so many of our problems. I'll leave the details regarding the damage they do for another day.

There is nothing evil about being financially independent. The individual who believes that money is at the root of all evil just flat-out doesn't have any. It is the lack of money that is at the root of all evil (George Bernard Shaw). Remember, the Bible does not say that money is the root of all evil. The Bible states, "It is *the love of money* which is at the root of all evil" (1 Timothy 6:10) [emphasis added].

Anyone who makes derogatory remarks toward another who is driving by in a $100,000 automobile is either envious or under the false pretense that all wealthy people got their bounty by illegal or immoral means. This is simply not so, and it is the trademark of the type of thought process that will keep you from becoming affluent yourself. That is a virtual guarantee.

Those who condemn wealth, besides not having any, are also blinded by the conviction that they have been dealt an unjust blow of fate. Nothing could be further from the truth as we've all had tough breaks and misfortune in our lives. This thinking has also led to the most dangerous political ideology, egalitarianism (engineered equality).

Many have adopted a Robin Hood mentality, doing their best to take from the rich and give to the poor in order to equalize the masses. Need, not achievement, has become the source of rights.

The unfortunate result is the proliferation of misguided civil rights movements that hope to achieve their ends with the utmost disregard for anybody or anything not in league with their cause. Because of this, American politics are being increasingly governed by special interest groups rather than by you and me. As leftist propaganda calls for equality for all, every minority subculture has jumped on the bandwagon, represented by their most vocal and extremist supporters.

Whether they are black civil rights leaders who wish to further their agenda at any cost, white supremacists, militant feminists, or the fringe groups of any minority, on the left or on the right, they are increasingly disinclined to take responsibility for their actions and lack of well-being. The resulting belief—that the world owes them a living—eventually leads to the creation of a welfare state.

Have we become totally blind? The grandest welfare experiment in the history of humanity has also been humanity's grandest failure. The entire socialist empire collapsed. It failed because it cannot work!

Let me expand on this last point. As wonderful as equality for all may sound, it fails every time because the individual loses his or her incentive to contribute. The greatest evil has often come from the desire to be virtuous, but the economies of egalitarianism simply do not work. When the desires of the few outweigh the needs of the many, then we have gone far beyond the original intent to protect the rights of the individual. The result is a form of reverse discrimination. It is now the average person's rights that are at risk because every minority known to man is being given preference rather than equality.

Equal opportunity has been tragically substituted with the quest for equality. Let's be honest: equality does not exist. We were not created equal, and it is an insult to think that we are all equal to one another as this would deny us our individuality. Besides, people do not want to be equal. They want to be rich.

Even with an increasing set of encumbrances, America is still the land of opportunity. So why is it that so few people have the knowledge that enables them to move toward prosperity? Maybe it's just not that easy to find. Consider the following example.

Britannica's sixty-volume Great Books series, when complemented by their encyclopedia, is considered one of Western civilization's crowning achievements. It is comprised of most of the great literary works of all time, including such authors as Aristotle, Aquinas, Shakespeare, Newton, Goethe, Tolstoy, and many others. This compilation of wisdom contains the best of what has been thought and written over the past twenty-five centuries.

Two of the volumes are called *The Syntopicon*, a self-proclaimed landmark achievement "in the history of intellectual life of this century." *The Syntopicon* isolates 102 topics that encompass the majority of the ideas and discussions that have been of concern to people over time. These ideas are common themes extracted from the Great Books.

It is the discussions that reappear multiple times in many of the great works of literature that have led to the idea of "The Great Conversation." The concept is one in which all the great scholars, philosophers, and scientists throughout history have engaged in a timeless conversation. The discussion has gone uninterrupted for 2,500 years and centers mostly around the aforementioned 102 topics.

One of those topics is wealth.

It is interesting to note that there is no attempt in the encyclopedia, in any of the Great Books, or in *The Syntopicon* to provide direction to show how an individual can accumulate wealth. There are a multitude of references to the theory, effects, and distribution of wealth, but no guide on how to attain wealth. There are even widespread discussions on how nations acquire wealth, but not individuals. Why was this left out?

What this means is that neither our greatest reference encyclopedia nor any of the most influential authors in history have attempted to define or compile any methods of wealth accumulation for individuals. From Homer and

Plato to Keynes and Adam Smith, no one has tried to methodically define one of our greatest day-to-day concerns, the quest for financial independence. This remains true even though wealthy individuals are often at the center of their plays, stories, theories, and discussions.

Is it any wonder that we don't know where to start? The principles of wealth have always been there, but no one has ever brought them together for us to follow.

I believe that one of the reasons for this discrepancy is that wealth created by an individual, as opposed to wealth resulting from inherited privileges, has until recently been unknown. Because an individual's earned wealth and his or her freedom cannot exist without each other, and widespread freedom is a recent phenomenon, so is personally created wealth. Therefore, although the principles of wealth are not new, their application is.

Do you want a German car, French food, Italian clothes, and American money? Do you want to own your own home? To offer your family security, vacations, and the best health care? Do you want to be a contributing member of society? Do you want the ability to do what you enjoy doing the most, whatever that may be? Do you want to be able to help others and claim your power to make a positive difference in the world?

You can have all the above. The answers you need are directly ahead.

You are about to discover how to use the tools made available to you in our free enterprise society. I do not claim originality for the principles outlined in this book. They are timeless. They were successful 5,000 years ago and will again be there to help our great-grandchildren and their children's children achieve success. My work is in bringing these truths together and presenting them in a methodical manner anyone can understand. They have been presented here to be relevant to current times as well as relevant into the next century. The principles of wealth should be used to help you contribute to the common good in our society.

If you succeed in creating wealth for yourself, be proud. It is the greatest distinction for any American. Americans were the first people to employ the concept of making money. No other nation has ever used the words "to make money" prior to ours.

According to Ayn Rand, author of *Atlas Shrugged,* "Men had always thought of wealth as a static quantity—to be seized, begged, inherited, looted or obtained as a favor. Americans were the first to understand that wealth has to be created. The words 'to make money' hold the essence of human morality. ... Wealth is the product of man's capacity to think."

The techniques and principles outlined in *The Secrets of Wealth* work in harmony with nature. That is their strength. As you shall see, they can even be found in nature, without mankind's intervention. Roman philosopher Seneca wrote, "True wisdom consists not in departing from nature but molding our conduct according to her laws and model."

The laws of abundance are the laws of nature.

Chapter 1:

The Quest for Knowledge

The Quest for Knowledge

"Knowledge is the currency of the universe."

Although it may seem obvious to some, it is important for everyone who reads this to understand that having money also means having a certain amount of power. To paraphrase Alvin Toffler in his book *Powershift*: we seek power to influence our environment and to provide ourselves with what we want and need. Rarely do we seek money for its own sake but rather for the power it holds for us.

Money is merely a tool, albeit a very powerful one. However, money is not the only form of power, not even the most "powerful." There are three distinctly separate forms of power available to us today: force (or the threat of force), money, and knowledge.

Force is the most primitive of the three and has been around as long as mankind. It involves the threat of violence to elicit action or to suppress action. In our modern society it is the source of power used by our police, government, and violent criminal elements.

For example, obedience to the law is based purely on this source of power. When a police officer tells us to follow his orders, he is backed by the threatened use of physical coercion. Likewise, when the courts enforce an action in a lawsuit, they do so by having the right to use force if we do not obey. The criminal may use it less subtly. At gunpoint, we have the choice to give him what he wants or risk being shot. The use of violence is hereby a form of negative reinforcement. Either we do something, or we will be punished.

Money is a more contemporary source of power. The origins of paper money can be traced back to the late Middle Ages where promissory notes could be used as an accepted means of exchange. It soon became more convenient to expand the use of these notes so that, rather than exchanging them for their underlying "cash," such as gold, the promissory notes themselves eventually became known as cash.

As we know it today, the concept of money came to America when the British Empire ordered their American colonists to stop using gold and silver coins as their means of exchange. The first Americans thus quickly learned to use paper money as a means of exerting purchasing power.

Modern paper money derives its value from the promise that it will be honored by another as legal tender. It lacks intrinsic value unless backed by hard assets, such as gold or silver. If it is not backed by hard assets (such as gold), it is called fiat money. Our acceptance of paper money is based purely on trusting that it will be accepted by another. Therefore paper money is backed only by our faith in the government (or its threatened use of force). Because our faith in government tends to be rather volatile, so is the value of our currency.

Money, unlike force, can be used positively and negatively. That is, someone can be punished by withholding money, or someone can be rewarded by receiving it. It is therefore a more flexible means of exerting power than the threat of force.

The disadvantage to both force and money is their finite nature. There is only so much of each that can be used at any one time. Too much force is counterproductive and eventually causes rebellion. There is a very well-defined limit before this happens, and one can hardly go far beyond this limit.

With money it is a little different. One can spend only a finite amount before going broke, but one can then resort to deficit spending, which allows the limits to be extended substantially beyond cash on hand.

Going into debt can be cleverly stretched to obscene limits. It can go far beyond the point of where one's deficit is secured by collateral. Unsecured debt has been the cause of numerous disasters for obvious reasons. Such a bubble cannot expand endlessly. Judgment day will come eventually. America is currently at its doorstep with a debt load that is clearly unsustainable.

Donald Trump also learned this lesson when he could no longer meet the interest payments on his over-leveraged real estate empire during the 1980s. The bubble burst, and he learned the hard way that money and credit have their limits.

Knowledge is the third source of power. It is not limited in the same ways that force and money are limited. Everybody can get more knowledge at any time, and everyone can use the same knowledge simultaneously. Furthermore, knowledge can be used by rich and poor people alike. One need only have the desire to find out where to look. The Internet has leveled the playing field for gaining most knowledge, but not all.

Knowledge has been replacing financial strength in our society as the primary source of power for quite some time now. Numerous best-selling books are available detailing this trend. The bottom line is that raw materials and manufacturing muscle will no longer be the primary source of advantage, employment, or wealth. But having the right knowledge will. We are increasingly becoming an information society.

Any way you measure it, knowledge is more strategically important than money because with knowledge you can get money. The correct use of knowledge is omnipotent in business, government, and in our personal lives. Even in a multibillion-dollar corporate buyout, it is the individual or group armed with superior knowledge that will win over those with more money almost every time.

Knowledge and information are also more strategically important than force. History is filled with tales of the weak overthrowing a larger force by applying superior knowledge of tactics or, in other words, having better information.

In current times, American armed forces have taken a quantum leap forward in the processing of information as initiated by the 1991 Gulf War. Our overwhelming superiority was not the result of a massive US armament buildup; it was the result of smart bombs. America introduced weapons that could process vast amounts of information to be effective far beyond their mere explosive capabilities. Their pinpoint accuracy ushered modern warfare into a new era.

Knowledge also plays a role in enabling us to make more efficient use of another finite commodity: time. Both time and money are limited to us. Have you ever noticed how we either have enough time or enough money but rarely both? Those who have lots of time are rarely affluent. Those who are affluent rarely have much time to spare. Hence the belief that time is money. The American dream is to have both—money and the time to enjoy it.

Though money and time may be equal in many ways, money, unlike time, cannot be wasted. It can be spent unwisely, but it cannot be wasted because it will always be somewhere after we spend it. Time can be wasted. Once spent, it is gone forever. It follows that if we waste time, we lose money. Having the right knowledge is the only way to ensure that we use our time efficiently. Henry

Ford was one of the first to articulate this and consequently invented the modern production line.

Consider the importance of time. It levels the playing field. Perfect equality exists in only this one area, the use of time. In this respect we are a perfect democracy. We all have equal opportunity to make use of our time in any way we want. No one can take it away from us to be redistributed, and we can waste it without fear of punishment. We all have all the time there is. No one can avoid the future; it waits no matter what you do. No one can alter the past; it has already happened. With time you cannot go into debt, and it cannot be withheld.

Owing time or taking away time are meaningless concepts as long as you remain free and healthy. It is only how we choose to use our time that makes us so very different. And that's where wealthy people differ the most from poor people, or even from nine-to-five employees. Wealthy people have learned to use their time more efficiently to generate income at levels not directly tied to the amount of time spent working. As they say, if you want to become wealthy, find out what poor people are doing with their time and then stop doing that.

Becoming dependent on information is changing our lives in ways that we can only begin to imagine. From the financial markets and defense industry down to the local supermarket and your home business, we have become an information society. Those who understand and use this knowledge will prosper now and far into the twenty-first century. Survival of the fittest is already taking on an entirely new meaning.

Our growing knowledge base is also taking on an entirely different structure than society has ever seen before. Those of us acquiring enough new knowledge to keep pace with current trends are doing so in increasingly specialized fields. That is, we are becoming experts in our particular field of interest. Ten, twenty, or thirty years ago it was much more fashionable to know a little about everything. With technology and information exploding in volume and complexity, this is no longer possible. We are now learning more and more about less and less. (Do we therefore risk eventually knowing everything about nothing?)

Knowledge is power, superior to force and money. Ironically, it follows that the most important piece of knowledge you can acquire is the understanding that knowledge is power. The bottom line is that you must never, never, never stop learning.

If you are to acquire wealth, you must arm yourself with the right information on how to do so. In fact, in line with recent trends toward specialization, you must strive to become an expert in your particular field. Relevant to this text, I am referring to thoroughly researching the specific path you will choose to arrive at financial independence.

The most successful individuals have taken this concept one step further. Since nothing is easier to learn than information surrounding your personal interests, it follows that you should either incorporate a passion into your financial future or, alternatively, make your wealth-building career your passion.

In the same way that sports buffs remember every piece of trivia surrounding sports, though they may have failed dismally in school, wealthy individuals generally enjoy the art of creating wealth more than anything else. This is their edge. They live and breathe what is both their career and their passion. Confucius said that if you choose a job you love, you will never have to work a day in your life.

After this text has fulfilled its promise of showing you step-by-step how financial independence can be obtained, it will be your continued thirst for more knowledge that will provide you with an impenetrable defense against failure.

Knowledge reduces or eliminates two undesirable aspects of building wealth: risk and fear. Knowledge will enable you to reduce your risks and allocate them wisely. The right knowledge will also keep you from fearing risk and the unknown. In fact, knowledge will empower you to welcome both. When risk and fear come under your control, you become unstoppable.

Recap:

- Knowledge is the highest form of power.

- Arm yourself with knowledge. Never stop learning.

- Become an expert in all aspects of your plan for financial independence.

In a previous section we examined how we must take economic matters into our own hands by creating wealth for ourselves if we are to contribute to keeping this nation on top. Besides our desire for the best life has to offer, it is also our duty to contribute economically. Let's recognize that becoming self-motivated to continually acquire more knowledge is another area where our own efforts seem to be our best alternative. Bluntly put, the level of education in this country is pathetic compared to the rest of the industrialized world, and nothing substantive is being done about it by those assigned with the task. Therefore we must solve the problem ourselves.

When comparing our students to international averages, we are first in only two categories: total hours spent watching television each day, and the amount of public expenditure per student. If publicly subsidized ignorance continues at this pace, America's current lack of competitiveness will reach epidemic proportions. Fully one quarter of all high school graduates each year are essentially illiterate. They couldn't even read George Bush's lips. Each of us bears some responsibility in this.

The origin of the issue is uniquely an American problem. Our complacency is largely the result of our attitude. First, the media and we are guilty of equating an educated youngster with a nerd. We have yet to make the connection between education and our economic future. Various subcultures within our borders, most notably

Asian Americans, are light-years ahead of us in this respect.

Americans also have a lingering belief that they are still God's gift to humanity because they were once undisputed world leaders. Americans had the strongest economy, the highest standard of living, the best opportunities for advanced education, and the most powerful military in the world. Well, no longer. The problem is, we are still not waking up to our shortfalls. We are the most self-righteous people in the Western Hemisphere.

Here is an example to illustrate my point: Americans believe that it is their God-given right to drive. This is witnessed by the ease with which anyone can obtain a driver's license in the United States. All it takes is about twenty dollars to register and an exam we can retake at any time if we don't get at least the equivalent of a "D" … and if we didn't take advantage of how easy it is to cheat during the exam.

Now let's ask ourselves why we have speed limits substantially below European averages? Germans do not have any speed limits at all. Is it to conserve gas, or is it to save lives? Maybe it's a bit of both, but there has to be another reason because accident rates are no higher in Germany than in America, and we certainly don't have a gas shortage.

The reason is that Americans, as a whole, don't know how to drive very well. They never learned properly. In

Europe it takes approximately three months of mandatory driving school before you're allowed to take a driving test, and the process costs about $2,000. If you fail, you're in for another three months of agony listening to your parents preaching to you about the wasted money. Therefore it is highly likely that the European student will learn how to drive safely from the start.

Driving in this country is considered a right, whereas in Europe it is a privilege and is treated as such. This same attitude also contributes to our faltering educational system. We are raised to think we're smart. Ask any high school dropout if he or she is prepared to compete with a Japanese worker. Their answer will be a self-righteous "of course."

This fallacy of American thought has a devastating impact on our economic well-being if left unchecked. We assume that widespread poverty is the result of a failed social support system, but we are missing the true cause: it is the direct result of our lack of education.

Only through education can the individual hope to provide the essential ingredient, productivity, to enable the move from poverty to wealth. Poverty is nonproductive, and wealth is not created without knowledge.

People are not born stupid; they are born uneducated. If this does not change as the individual matures, he or she will never have the tools to make use of his or her greatest asset, a thinking brain.

This country needs change. Change is the result of creative thought, but creative thought cannot spring from an untrained mind. The means to create is missing.

An ignorant society also creates a self-defeating by-product. It creates government agencies whose function is to protect the "unfortunate" from being preyed upon by the more educated echelons. This is another misguided and wasteful attempt that ignores the real problem, lack of education. If we redirected our energies into educating our public, we wouldn't have to feel like they need to be protected. They could easily protect themselves.

The proliferation of an obscene number of consumer protection agencies is a clear danger sign pointing in the direction of Big Brother. We are simply throwing away the means to take care of ourselves. Unfortunately this is due in part to an intentional leftist agenda in this country that can thrive only if there is a widespread belief that we need help and protection, from others and from ourselves. Government has been cleverly positioned to be our savior. What a frightening thought.

Our first step is to change some of the destructive attitudes that got us into this mess. Let's drop the false pretense that we are fully prepared for any challenge, whether it's foreign competition or a personal quest. We are not. But there is a bright side. Ignorance is a curable disease. So let's do something about it.

The one asset we all possess is the potential to become equal to the fortunate few. We were obviously not born that way. Sorry to contradict you, President Jefferson, but all men are not created equal (maybe you meant cremated equal). Only if we all contribute can we improve the level of education all around us. We must do this also as a prerequisite to creating widespread wealth.

Where do we start? We start with the one we see in the mirror. To create wealth we must first educate ourselves. We must acquire knowledge—for our sake, for our children's sake, for everyone's sake.

How does one acquire knowledge outside conventional schooling facilities? Here is the greatest wealth-building and educational tool available to anyone willing to make the effort: read. Read books, read magazines, read newsletters. Every question we could possibly ask is answered in a book somewhere. There are answers available to questions we haven't even dreamed of yet. It is true that "we don't know all the things that we don't know." We just need to open our eyes to the vast amounts of information contained in books and learn.

You can find a book on anything. Recently I even saw a book titled *How to Read a Book*. Reading is one of the most profitable pastimes you can indulge in. Every leader is a reader. That's a fact. Unless you read, you will not succeed.

Mark Twain said, "The man who doesn't read good books has no advantage over the man who can't read them." In my opinion that says it all.

Reading is an investment that pays healthy dividends. How much should we invest? If you invest 2 percent of your income in quality learning tools, you will never be unemployed again, and your income will rise—guaranteed. There is a plethora of self-help books to choose from in any bookstore, library, or on the Internet. There are quality books available on any imaginable subject. Additionally, audio recordings of books enable us to make use of our idle time. Most of us drive from 12,000 to 25,000 miles each year. Listening to an educational "book on tape" while commuting is not only productive, it can also be very enjoyable.

Educating yourself is not expensive. Ignorance is. If you genuinely don't have the money to spend on this critical investment, do not despair. Any decent public library offers books, CDs, and even videos. Their use is free, so there is no excuse for not taking advantage of these tools. If you believe you cannot afford to spend the time to read, let me tell you, you can't afford not to.

"When I get a little money, I buy books; and if any is left, I buy food and clothes."

–Desiderius Erasmus

Chapter 2:

The Spending Law

The Spending Law

Have you ever noticed how the vast majority of people around you are living paycheck to paycheck, regardless of their income? This includes people making many thousands of dollars per month.

The reason relates to the second truth to be discovered, which may actually be one of the greatest mysteries in the world. It states that for the vast majority of people, your expenses will always equal or surpass your income, regardless of how small or how large that income may be.

If you were to ask an auditorium full of average people how many of them truthfully feel they are on a lean budget, virtually everyone would raise their hand. Yet everyone cannot be earning the same amount of money. In other words, according to the law of expenses, almost everyone always feels that money is tight.

The truth behind this statement will not be evident until you are well on your journey to acquiring financial independence. As your income grows, you will notice that your expenses will expand and multiply to match or even outpace your increase in earnings. And your expenses will do this as if they had a mind of their own.

Consider this: During my college days my total net income was about $600 per month. As little as it may seem, it did meet my expenses. In retrospect, I now know that it was my expenses that met my income, not the other way around. Repeatedly I had the thought that if I could make only a few hundred dollars more per month, I would be able to live in relative comfort and still be able to afford some of life's minor luxuries.

It did not take long for me to earn those extra few hundred dollars, but they did not seem to make much difference. Granted, I no longer had to eat $1 slices of New York pizza for breakfast, lunch, and dinner, but the relief I expected never materialized. Financial fulfillment had seemed no farther away than being able to afford breakfast at my favorite sidewalk cafe in Venice Beach, California, before going to work every day.

I later gained employment in a Fortune 1000 company, MCI Communications, earning the unbelievable sum of $1,200 per month. I felt as if I was going to be on top of the world. I would now even be able to save money, an activity that has always been very dear to my heart. But then something quite mysterious happened to me. My expenses quickly went up to $1,200 per month. Baffled, I searched for the source of my extravagance. I totaled all the bills covering my basic necessities and discovered the number was the same as my income. Somehow it seemed that my expenditures knew about my raise and conspired to raise my cost of living by an amount equal to my increase. Some bills grew, and then there were new ones, appearing from out of nowhere. Nonetheless, upon careful examination I found that even my new monthly debts were apparently essential to my modest lifestyle.

My lesson in adulthood was countered with fierce determination to outpace the economic conspiracy that was threatening to keep me from personal stardom. I needed to make more money.

My earnings did increase within a reasonably short period of time, but I had no luck stretching my dollars any further than I always had. Distraught, I looked around and found that I was fortunate compared to many others. Their expenditures were substantially outpacing their income. At least I was not in debt.

As my life progressed, I have to honestly say that my lifestyle improved quite substantially. Admittedly, I even had a close encounter of the yuppie kind. During my mid to late twenties, I witnessed a reevaluation of the financial enigma also plaguing each of my acquaintances. As our incomes increased, so would our dues. It never seemed to approach the point of excess cash, no matter what we did or how much we earned. Regardless of our savings accounts, secret compartments in our mattresses, or repeated attempts at get-rich-quick schemes, we were all in the same boat trying to paddle upstream. The financial waterfall we were trying to escape promised to throw us into an economic stalemate. We had no cushion for a rainy day.

As Mark Twain once wisely stated, "Youth is wasted on the young." So quite a few years later and a hundred years smarter, I finally figured it out. Let me try to explain what was happening by using an analogy involving taxes. Taxes provide a useful model for understanding the "Money coming in equals money going out" law.

As our income increases, the amount of our tax liability also increases. Taxes are progressive. That is, the *percentage* of income that taxes eliminate from our paycheck increases as our income increases. Hence we have tax brackets. To add to the misery of taxation, as we enter higher income brackets, we are also hit with entirely new sources of taxes specifically designed to soak the rich, only the government's definition of "rich" is a lot lower than your or my definition of "rich." These new taxes are analogous to the previously mentioned new expenses appearing from out of nowhere.

Our expenses appear to increase in the same way taxes do. For example, if your income increases and you can afford a bigger apartment, then all expenses associated with your new lifestyle will be higher in proportion to the size of your new residence. Both utilities and rent will obviously increase. Even your food costs will go up as you can now afford better quality food. This all happens without much thought on our part. In fact, it typically happens without *any* thought on our part. The point is, expenses tend to also be progressive in nature.

Beyond taxes and other unavoidable expenses such as rent and utilities, there is another money drain responsible for our conundrum. This one is very important to understand because there is something we can do about it. It is the need we feel to dump our earnings into some nonessential expenses we feel are quite necessary, or at the very least, that we feel we richly deserve based on our new level of income. These are also the expenses that mysteriously appear from out of nowhere every time we think we have progressed somewhat financially. Once we become accustomed to these, which I do not define as superfluous luxuries, they are extremely hard to reverse by sheer willpower. However, if our income were to suddenly decline, these would be the first expenses to disappear.

For our current discussion, let's call these expenses "secondary expenses" with the understanding that they are not unnecessary luxuries nor are they absolute necessities. If removed, chances are we would rarely miss these outlays as much as one would assume. But since most of us suffer from a chronic inability to distinguish between need and greed, they are very quick to reappear if we become careless.

We will work with these secondary expenses later in our plan as they afford us a tremendous opportunity.

It should be noted that everyone has some secondary expenses, regardless of how low their income is. Even the transient on the street spends money on cigarettes and/or alcohol, both of which fall into this category.

Recap:

- Our expenses will always equal our income. As our income rises, so will our expenses rise to meet our new income.

- Ordinary expenses that are neither superfluous luxuries nor vital expenditures to sustain basic life are secondary expenses.

Chapter 3:

Spend More Money

Spend More Money!

If we assume that those expenses that aren't 100 percent essential to our livelihood are secondary expenses, then we can call those having first claim to our income primary expenses. Thus, if one makes X dollars per month, the first checks written by any responsible person go to pay for primary expenses. These include basic necessities such as food, shelter, utilities, and transportation.

It is the knowledge of how our expenses behave in relation to our income that provides us with a tremendous opportunity.

When we talk about our primary and secondary expenses, we refer to them as our bills. Every month, we religiously sit down to pay our bills. Here's the irony: We order the prettiest checks available with lots of flowers and bright ornaments to send to our creditors. We do this for the people we like least in the world, the ones getting our money instead of us. Now ask yourself why do all of your creditors have first claim to your money? It's your money! You worked for it, you earned it, yet you don't get to keep any of it. Something is definitely wrong here.

If you are thinking ahead and pondering whether I'm about to advocate not paying your bills so that you get to keep your money, let me assure you right now, that is not so. What we are going to do is manipulate your expenditures a little. We're going to add a bill to your list. The beneficiary of that bill is you—yes, YOU! Not only are we going to add a bill, we're going to make it the first bill you pay. It will be the primary expense of all primary expenses. You will actually write yourself a check every time you get paid.

The amount you pay yourself has to be at least 10 percent of your earnings. This is very important. It is the first concrete step in our plan toward financial independence. If you can afford more than 10 percent, then you will achieve your goals more quickly. Write a check to yourself every time you get paid. Do it before you write any other, even if you don't see how you are going to make ends meet. Trust me—your lifestyle will not change significantly.

As you continue to pay yourself 10 percent of all the monies you earn, you must never, never, never miss a payment to yourself. If you do, you will have sold out and you will fail. Period. You must pay yourself religiously. Temptation will be waiting for you to cheat. Not only will you be tempted to miss a payment here and there, promising that you'll make it up later, but there is an even greater evil lurking around the corner waiting to throw you back into a mediocre lifestyle.

After a few payments you will soon be tempted to dip into your savings. This will happen for very specific reasons. After several months of accumulating 10 percent or more of what you earn, if you are like most people, you will have at your disposal more money than you are usually accustomed to. You have been living from paycheck to paycheck, and this is new territory for you.

After those initial months of steadfast saving, you will suddenly be very pleased with your progress and performance. At that point you will want to reward yourself with that pretty new dress you saw in the window, or a new stereo, or the latest iPhone or purse, or whatever else you may fancy. You must resist. Your savings become your seed money that will catapult you toward a thousand dresses, stereos, or—more simply— wealth. If you touch your savings now, you will fail.

A short summary will recap this phase of our plan:

- Add a bill to your list of primary expenses, i.e., pay yourself at least 10 percent of your income. Make it your first payment and segregate this money into its own bank account. That is, keep it separate from your regular checking account.

- NEVER skip a payment to yourself!

- Do not dip into your savings even when they start to grow into substantial amounts of money.

Here is the key to the entire strategy. It is important to understand that you will not miss the 10 percent of your earnings you are now saving. As hard as it may be to believe, you will not realize the truth behind this claim until you try. It has been demonstrated many times. The increasing popularity of biweekly mortgage payments can help to illustrate this.

Biweekly mortgage programs consist of making a payment equal to one half of a regular mortgage payment every two weeks rather than a full payment every month. Thus you will make twenty-six half payments per year instead of twelve full payments. Because twenty-six half payments, or twenty-six two-week periods, is the equivalent of thirteen months instead of the customary twelve monthly payments, you will make an extra full month's payment each year.

The extra two half payments are applied to the principal of your loan, not the interest. Over the years this drastically reduces the amount of your obligation and the time it takes to pay off your loan. You will save a significant portion of the interest, often tens or hundreds of thousands of dollars depending on your loan size and interest rate, by paying off some of the principal early. Additionally you will pay off your loan years early.

Here's where we're going with this: If you are a homeowner, the important aspect of the biweekly mortgage strategy is the minimal impact it has on your lifestyle. Making an extra mortgage payment every year will hardly be felt. There's a reason for this. Because most months are longer than four weeks, the net effect of what you are doing is accelerating your monthly payments by a few days every month. You will effectively be making a full payment every four weeks instead of every month. To most people this is hardly worth mentioning.

The 10 percent savings rule has a similar insignificant effect on your lifestyle. What will happen is that one or more of your secondary expenses will simply fade away or be reduced. This is usually quite automatic. Astonishingly, you will find that you really will not miss whatever it is you are eliminating from your life. As explained earlier, this holds true even if your total income is meager.

When I first discovered the 10 percent rule, I suspected that it had not simply been made up randomly by someone long ago. It seemed to have a much more significant origin. Even today, as I watch other people read about it for their first time, I often hear that they intuitively knew this is what they should have been doing all along.

In fact, the 10 percent rule does have an ancient origin. Its significance was well recognized even before the time of Moses. It originates from the word "tithe," which means "a tenth." Hence we have the word "tithing," meaning "to give," or more accurately, "to give a tenth."

Saving 10 percent of your income is the same as putting aside more than one entire month's income every year. It's like having an extra paycheck. Year after year this alone has the potential to work wonders for your future. All it takes is for you to try it.

If you still don't believe that you can save 10 percent of your income, consider this scenario. What if you had a nine-to-five job and the company you worked for started doing less well as a result of a recession? Unemployment is on the rise and the thought of having to find a new job is scary because it might be nearly impossible in the current economic environment. Now your manager comes to your department and tells you that he has been given the directive to reduce expenses by 10 percent in order to keep the company alive.

Your manager has two choices. One is to terminate 10 percent of the workforce, which might include anyone in the room, including you. The other is for everyone to take a 10 percent pay cut. Which would you choose? Do you think you could survive on 10 percent less money if the alternative is the possibility of being fired and having no pay at all? You know the answer. Everyone would opt for the 10 percent pay cut and make it work without too much difficulty. In fact, given the parameters and choices above, it is a small price to pay.

Saving 10 percent is only the beginning. Next, I'll show you what to do with your savings.

Chapter 4:

Sit Back, Relax, Get Rich

Sit Back, Relax, Get Rich

You have been told not to spend your savings. What then are we saving for if not to spend? Well, we are saving to spend, but not quite on what you may think. We must spend wisely; that is, we must invest our money.

Investing simply means that you're using your money to earn more money. Every dollar you earn is like a worker that can help you earn more dollars. It only has to be put to work effectively. Its earnings, in turn, can earn even more money. This is called *compounding your interest*, allowing your earned money to earn more money for you.

Please reread the preceding paragraph again until its meaning sinks in. It is very important that you fully understand what it means to compound your interest.

Ultimately, when you have enough money in your pool of capital to live comfortably off the money that it is earning without touching your primary pool of capital, then you will be financially wealthy. This can be achieved through the power of compounding alone.

The next step is to acquire the knowledge of how fruitful compounding can be if understood and used correctly. Let me illustrate with a classic example.

If I offered you the choice of receiving $1,000 every day for thirty days, or one cent on the first day, doubled on the second (two cents), doubled again on the third (four cents), etc. for thirty days, which would you choose?

In the first scenario, you know you will end up with $30,000 after thirty days. In the second scenario, what is happening? In financial terms your money is receiving 100 percent interest every day. That is, you are receiving 100 percent daily appreciation on your principal, one cent, and on the interest it is earning every day. 100 percent interest means your money doubles every day. It is actually compounding at 100 percent every day.

Obviously earning 100 percent interest is not a realistic investment potential, but it serves to illustrate the power of compounding as most people would choose the first scenario. It provides a very predictable return over the thirty days in our example, $30,000.

Let's put each version side by side to compare. The numbers show the total amount that you have accumulated on a given day in each scenario.

DAY	VERSION 1	VERSION 2
1	$ 1,000.00	$ .01
2	$ 2,000.00	$ .02
3	$ 3,000.00	$ .04
4	$ 4,000.00	$ .08
5	$ 5,000.00	$ .16
6	$ 6,000.00	$ .32
7	$ 7,000.00	$ .64
8	$ 8,000.00	$ 1.28
9	$ 9,000.00	$ 2.56
10	$ 10,000.00	$ 5.12

Would you still choose Version 1? Probably. Most people do.

11	$ 11,000.00	$ 10.24
12	$ 12,000.00	$ 20.48
13	$ 13,000.00	$ 40.96
14	$ 14,000.00	$ 81.92
15	$ 15,000.00	$ 163.84
16	$ 16,000.00	$ 327.68
17	$ 17,000.00	$ 655.36
18	$ 18,000.00	$ 1310.72
19	$ 19,000.00	$ 2621.44
20	$ 20,000.00	$ 5242.88

How about now? Do you see what is happening?

21	$ 21,000.00	$ 10,485.76
22	$ 22,000.00	$ 20,971.52
23	$ 23,000.00	$ 41,943.04
24	$ 24,000.00	$ 83,886.08
25	$ 25,000.00	$ 167,772.16
26	$ 26,000.00	$ 335,544.32
27	$ 27,000.00	$ 671,088.64
28	$ 28,000.00	$ 1,342,177.28
29	$ 29,000.00	$ 2,684,354.56
30	$ 30,000.00	$ 5,368,709.12
Totals	**$ 30,000.00**	**$ 5,368,709.12**

How about now?

This is the power of compounding!

After just thirty days, you will have over $5 million in the compounded example! In Version 1 you end up with a mere $30,000. This is why one of the Rothschilds called compounding "The Eighth Wonder of the World."

It is obvious that there is no investment in the world that will provide this kind of return. A 100 percent return compounded daily would be quite the fantasy, but this example does serve to illustrate several important points.

First, compounding is an extremely powerful investment strategy. You will shortly see how compounding your money can work miracles for you, even at much lower rates of interest.

Secondly, it is important to note that the average person's investment mentality is hopelessly stuck in our Version 1. It is also precisely the reason why ordinary savings do not work to pull us out of our everyday routine. *The dollars we save are simply not working for us.*

Finally, we can now discuss why it is so important to never dip into your savings or capital while it is growing. Imagine what a devastating effect it would have in our compounded version if we were to spend just $100 on day fifteen of our investment adventure. That $100 represents over half our total capital. Even if it's just a hundred bucks, this would effectively destroy the final results after thirty days, cutting it down to less than half the total. Conversely, the effect of spending $100,000 every day after day twenty-eight would hardly be felt.

Patience is the key. Compounding takes time.

Here is a nonfinancial analogy to further illustrate the importance of the early stages of compounded growth. Assume you have a company with one hundred employees and one of them quits. Does this impact your company's productivity? Probably not as you would simply shift their workload to several coworkers and go on with your business. One person leaving a workforce out of a hundred workers is just not a big deal.

Now assume your company is still in its infancy and has only two employees. One of them quits. Now you have a problem, a serious problem. Half your workforce just walked out on you, and your company could suffer irreparable damage as a result. The early stages of your company's growth are dramatically more vulnerable. It is the same with your investments.

Likewise, during the beginning stages of your business's growth, you do not want to take any time off because each day can witness a significant advance or a severe setback. The ups and downs are much more extreme during this stage because you have not yet reached a point of production and earnings stability. Once your revenues are up and you have more employees, that's when you may consider a vacation. This is entirely similar to dipping into your savings too soon because the risks are all in the early years. Once again, patience and discipline are your most important assets.

Back to our thirty-day example. Those of you thinking ahead will also deduce that starting with a larger capital base will have a tremendously advantageous effect, especially toward the end. Try playing with the numbers yourself. Instead of starting with one cent, start with $100 or even $1,000. See how far you get before running out of digits on your calculator.

Those of you who already have a little pool of savings stashed away somewhere probably do not realize how much potential is locked up in that cookie jar.

Recap:

- Invest your savings so that they can go to work for you.

- The best way to invest is by compounding your interest. This simply means reinvesting your earned interest to earn more interest for you.

- Never, ever dip into your pool of capital until the power of compounding has fulfilled its goal of making you a fortune.

One of the best books to describe the virtues of using the 10 percent rule and reinvesting the income in a compounding vehicle to accumulate wealth is *The Richest Man in Babylon* by George S. Clason. It was written in

1926. In this timeless story, a man named Arkad was told by Algamish, his tutor, "You do eat the children of your savings. Then how do you expect them to work for you? And how can they have children that will also work for you? First, get thee an army of golden slaves and then many a rich banquet may you enjoy without regret."

Chapter 5:

You Can Lift the World

You Can Lift the World

Archimedes, the Greek mathematician and physicist, once said that if he had a lever long enough and a pivot behind which he could stand, he alone could lift the world. In theory his statement is true. What Archimedes was referring to is the power of leverage, and it is the next financial tool we have at our disposal. In our plan we will put it into action after paying yourself first (saving), after investing, and after compounding your earnings. Some people may change the order depending on their means, tolerance of risk, and financial goals. Nonetheless, leverage is another universal financial principal that has awesome power and potential.

Whereas the amazing potential of compounding is revealed over time, leverage can work very quickly to multiply your money.

Leverage is the art of multiplying your input to provide a much greater output. When we use a lever to move a heavy boulder, we are using leverage. The long end of the lever moves through a greater distance than the short end, but the short end generates more power. Distance and force are related. If one is great, then the other is small. Great distance combined with little exerted power on the input side translates into short distance with great released power on the output side.

Pulleys work on the same principle. A heavy mass is lifted by a very modest amount of strength where the output side moves through a shorter distance than the input side. The input side moves through a greater distance but requires very little force.

Financial leverage is similar. We use a small amount of money to control a much larger amount. Invested properly, the profit will be in proportion to the larger sum being controlled rather than the smaller amount we invested. This is because the profit is generated by the whole amount we control.

For example, when a commodities trader controls $100,000 worth of gold with only $10,000, he is using leverage. His profit will come from the entire $100,000, as if he had paid for all the gold.

Financial leverage is made possible by using other people's money, borrowed money. Thus, in our previous example, the investor provides $10,000 and borrows the remaining $90,000. The $10,000 acts as the minimum acceptable down payment as determined by the lender. It acts as good faith money in case the investment turns against the trader, and it shows fiscal responsibility during the transaction. With a $10,000 down payment and $90,000 borrowed, the investor then controls $100,000 worth of gold.

The use of leverage may also carry substantial risks if used incorrectly. When trading in futures contracts on the commodities exchange for example, the leverage you get from multiplying your profits may also translate into multiplying your losses should your investment go the wrong way. It may even cause you to lose more than you initially invested. This is because the profit as well as the losses comes from the whole investment amount, not just the down payment amount. Thus, if the same investment is not monitored skillfully and is allowed to decline in value by half, for example, the investor loses $50,000. Though his deposit was only $10,000, he still has to make up the $40,000 difference. This is essentially a devastating 500 percent loss, five times more than the investor put in.

The preceding scenario will be of little concern to us because our use of leverage will be limited to the safest of all investment instruments. The volatility inherent in futures contracts is to be avoided at all costs. The profit potential is not worth the risk. It is, however, important to understand how leverage in its purest form can cause disaster for the unwary as easily as it can create staggering profits.

Nonetheless, one way to reduce risk in investments such as commodities and yet still have the potential of a leveraged upside is through options. When buying an option, the upside potential is similar to a futures contract, but your risk is limited to the amount you invest. Unlike commodities futures, options have time limits. Therefore, if your option does not appreciate within the allotted time, it will simply expire and you will lose your entire investment, but no more.

The principles and techniques of using leverage can get tremendously complex. Shrewd investors are continuously coming up with complex new ways to make leverage work for them. But our use of leverage is not only easy to learn and understand, it is also extremely safe.

The area in which we will use leverage has been around for ages and is familiar to us all. That area is real estate. This is the area we will explore as the upside potential is vastly greater than most people realize, yet the downside is limited because in the end you still own a piece of real estate that eventually will recoup any temporary losses. History has proven this many times over because real estate has intrinsic value that makes it substantially more secure. That is also why it has been said that the most valuable investment on Earth is earth.

For our purposes it will suffice to gain a basic understanding of how leverage is applied in real estate investments without getting lost in the countless different strategies available to the savvy real estate speculator.

Real estate investments are usually financed in part because the price of property is so high. The amount financed in the form of a mortgage provides the leverage we seek.

An important aspect to a leveraged real estate investment is the ease of entry into the market. It does not require vast sums of money, nor are the requirements excessively stringent. But you will still have the power of leverage on your side.

There are typically several lending institutions with exceptionally low entry requirements. The traditional 10 to 20 percent down payment is sometimes reduced to zero. That's right—depending on market conditions, you can sometimes buy real estate with nothing down. Because purchase requirements are ever changing, you have to see what is currently available. This does not, however, interfere with your ability to use leverage because requirements are always reasonable enough that you can buy real estate with a modest down payment in relation to the value of the entire property.

Real estate has been made significantly more affordable than most people realize. Because real estate is considered a low-risk investment for borrower and lender alike, institutions and individuals are continually devising new methods to make its potential work for them.

In Japan, for example, the exorbitant cost of property has led to the creation of ultra-leveraged purchases with 100-year mortgages. These mortgages may not be paid off for generations as property debts are passed on from parent to child. The standard length for a mortgage in the US is thirty years with some homeowners opting for a fifteen-year term if they can afford the higher monthly payment.

Assuming your whole life's savings amounts to only $20,000, this is often enough to purchase a property worth many times that amount, assuming you have decent credit and verifiable income—and even those are not always required. Thousands of Americans have purchased beautiful homes with even less, so don't worry if you do not yet have $20,000. This book will show you how to get it in a later chapter.

More important than the low capital requirements is the relative ease with which the average person can qualify for a mortgage loan. This applies even if you do not have years of stellar credit history. The reason is that mortgage loans are secured loans. That is, the property being purchased acts as collateral to the loan. If the buyer should suddenly stop making payments, the property defaults into the hands of the lender. The lender can then resell it to recoup their losses.

Contrary to popular belief, most banks and lending institutions do very much want to provide mortgage loans, and they want you to keep your property by making timely payments. Lending institutions are not in the business of repossessing properties from borrowers in dire straits.

To illustrate how leverage works in real estate, let's examine a case where Stephen Smith has $20,000 to invest in either a business or in a property. The options are as follows:

- Buying a $20,000 business for $20,000

- Buying a $100,000 home with $20,000 down and getting a mortgage for the remaining $80,000 balance

Purchasing the business provides Stephen with no leverage, whereas buying the home provides him with 80 percent leverage (80 percent of the purchase price of the home is borrowed).

Let's further assume that both investments appreciate 10 percent in value over the course of a single year. The business will therefore increase in value by $2,000 (10 percent of $20,000) and the house will gain in value by $10,000 (10 percent of $100,000).

Already we see an imbalance. The property investment has increased in value five times as much as the business although both appreciated by an equal 10 percent. Remember that both investments began with the same amount, $20,000.

To express the preceding example in financial terms, the non-leveraged investment, the business, earned a 10 percent return, whether it's from profit or an increase in the business's value. When $2,000 is earned from $20,000, it is a 10 percent return on investment.

The leveraged home purchase earned a 50 percent return because $10,000 earned from $20,000 is a 50 percent return on investment.

The power of leverage is obvious in this example: there are two investments, both of which were $20,000, and both of which earned a 10 percent return on the total value of the asset they represent. Yet the leveraged investment earned five times as much money as the non-leveraged investment because the appreciation is on the entire value.

To illustrate:

	Business	**Property**
Initial investment	$20,000	$20,000
Value	$20,000	$100,000
Amount borrowed	None	$80,000
Leverage	None	80%
Appreciation after one year	10%	10%
Profit	$2,000	$10,000
Return on initial investment	10%	50%

There is an endless variety of real estate transactions one can make. They range from buying a home with no money down to commercial properties and income-producing rental properties. Your choice will depend on your education in the field, your means, and your experience. Ultimately what matters is making an informed decision about the investment you choose.

Most will start with the purchase of the home that will become their residence. But even then it needs to be an informed decision. You need to become educated in the areas that involve answers to the following questions: Is the home in an area that has appreciation potential? Are you buying the home at or below its fair market price? Is the real estate market in a growth cycle and not near the top where prices may likely decline temporarily in the near future?

To tie the two previous chapters on compounding and leverage together, imagine the awesome potential of an investment strategy that combines these two tools. Better yet, what if these two vehicles could work for you automatically? They can. For example, if a leveraged real estate investment appreciates 10 percent for multiple years, it is also compounding at the same time. In the first year, you will earn 10 percent of the value of the property, bringing its new value to 110 percent of the original amount. In the second year you will earn 10 percent on the new value of the property. Thus, you earn "interest on your interest," in addition to your principal. Since the principal is leveraged, the profit potential is staggering provided it is allowed enough time to work.

Here are some numbers to show you what I mean. Let's assume you invest $10,000 in real estate, and this represents a 10 percent down payment, Let's further assume the property appreciates 10 percent per year—optimistic but historically not impossible. Therefore, the property is worth $100,000 when you buy it, and it will gain $10,000 in value the first year. That's 100 percent appreciation on your investment in one year! But what happens if the property continues to appreciate at the same rate of 10 percent each year?

In ten years the property will be worth $259,375. If you subtract the amount of the original mortgage loan ($90,000), you are left with an equity of $169,375. Here, in the real world, your original $10,000 compounded annually until it became $169,375 in only ten years!

Recap:

- Leveraging is the art of multiplying your input to provide a much greater output.

- Real estate provides one of the safest forms of leveraged investments.

- Real estate is a secured investment. It is therefore relatively easy for most people to qualify for a mortgage loan.

- Real estate investments do not require huge sums of money.

- Real estate is also a compounding investment. It thus provides an awesome profit potential by combining two of the principles of wealth creation we have examined thus far.

- Research and knowledge are the keys to making the correct choices in real estate.

The secret to the power of financial leverage is this: leverage is debt. Debt is borrowed money. That is, you are using other people's money. It is the wise use of borrowed money that allows your wealth to accumulate at a pace that simply cannot be matched anywhere else. Most wealthy individuals have learned to love debt. They understand that liabilities, used responsibly, can be their greatest asset.

Consider the benefits of debt. Whatever it is you need that you don't have, especially capital, someone has it who is willing to lend it to you. Using your own money may sound virtuous, but it's not always smart, not if you want to make a killing. If you can borrow ten times more money than you have yourself, your earnings have the potential of being ten times greater. Debt, when used in combination with low-risk investments is completely different from the disasters resulting from excessive consumer debt. It is used to create wealth, unlike credit cards that help to destroy it.

Moving on, leverage with an acceptable level of risk is not limited to real estate. Let's assume you want to leverage the purchase of a new business. That is, you want to borrow part of the purchase capital. Financing can be obtained in a variety of ways depending on how the funds are to be used. There are banks, mortgage lenders who provide lines of credit, venture capital firms, the Small Business Administration, and a variety of other government agencies specifically created to provide financing. However, these are not always your best choices, except maybe for a line of credit on your home. One of the most common sources of financing, especially for new business start-ups, often remains unmentioned. It is private financing from an individual.

This country is filled with affluent individuals seeking to invest their liquid assets by funding promising new projects. These individuals, commonly called angel investors or just angels, are typically approached by a friend, acquaintance, or family member, and asked to invest. But don't expect them to knock on your door because they probably have no clue about your business plans. You have to knock on theirs and tell them why your business would be a great home for their money.

The advantages to using a private investor are numerous. First, they generally base their decision on their trust in your abilities, your passion, and your willingness to share in the risk. Banks and venture capital firms do exactly the opposite. They couldn't care less if your iron determination is your guarantee against failure. They want credit history, business plans, and application forms—lots of application forms. They will also fund only certain types of ventures, and ironically, they often want to see that you really don't need the money. Only then will they give it to you.

Private investors are different. They generally do not breathe down your neck at the first hint of trouble, they do not always require collateral, and they offer you much more autonomy. More importantly, they can be a solid source of advice. They may even become your mentor.

Private investors are successful themselves. Therefore they've probably already made all the mistakes. Their knowledge is worth more to you than sitting through four years of business school. Their knowledge and the lessons they have learned are real world, not theory. So in addition to start-up capital, you may receive something much more valuable than money from a private investor, qualified advice and guidance.

Most successful individuals want to be someone's mentor. It's their way of giving back. Bankers and loan agents may have no clue as to the realities of your business enterprise. They are administrative employees. Their experience is therefore often severely limited. To find your angel, look around, ask around, and then plan your approach. It never hurts to ask. You may be surprised.

Chapter 6:

The Plan

The Plan

As promised, you will now be provided with the necessary details to propel you toward financial freedom. These are step-by-step instructions that will assume minimum starting capital requirements, the equivalent of a medium-paying job as a source of income, and the knowledge contained in this book.

This chapter is a raw outline of how to apply the principles of wealth accumulation that we have explored. This chapter does not tell you, however, where to place your funds for an acceptable compounded return or the specifics on how to make leveraged real estate work for you. That will happen in a subsequent chapter. At this point we are still discussing theory, albeit in a practical, step-by-step way.

This chapter's information is timeless. It does not matter what decade we are in as these are principles that have been around for thousands of years and will continue to remain valid. On the other hand, the information on where to achieve compounded returns and how to best apply leverage is forever changing. Nonetheless, the types of investments I will describe shortly should remain valid for a long time also—as long as the basics of our current financial system do not change dramatically.

There are many paths one may follow using our principles, not just the ones we will discuss in this book. As mentioned before, these financial principles are not only timeless, but they are also universal. That is, they have far-reaching applications in all areas of our lives, financial and otherwise.

Let's get started.

Step #1: Remove at least 10 percent of your income before you spend it on anything else. Do this with every paycheck and with every source of funds you receive, and do this every time you receive those monies. Do this religiously. With every paycheck, your first payment will be to yourself. Pay yourself before you pay rent, utilities, or anything else. NEVER miss a payment to yourself. Remember that the only likely change to your financial situation and lifestyle is that the monies you pay yourself will simply remove and replace one or more of your secondary expenses. This is rarely noticed to any significant degree. Your primary expenses will remain untouched.

Step #2: Place the 10 percent into a separate savings or checking account. Do not comingle these funds with any other funds.

Step #3: Once you have accumulated a few months' savings, place the entire amount into an investment vehicle that allows you to compound your money. We'll discuss which compounding investments to choose from in a subsequent chapter. Once you have opened your compounding investment, your ongoing 10 percent payment to yourself should go directly into your compounding investment, adding to and growing the principal every month. By saving and investing in this way, you will build a sizable nest egg very quickly, even without compounding. NEVER dip into this fund.

The frequent deposits you make will cause your savings to grow steadily. If you add the compounding effect to the interest you earn, you will eventually make your savings multiply. Regular savings versus a compounded savings plan will demonstrate to you in real life the difference between linear growth and exponential growth. It was illustrated in our thirty-day compounding example in the chapter titled "Sit Back, Relax, Get Rich."

Investment vehicles that compound your interest are all around us, but all are not created equal. We must seek one that compounds frequently (at least monthly) and that also provides an acceptable interest rate. It must also be very safe. These criteria provide us with a minimum acceptable standard.

Step #4: Let your capital grow. This will provide some of the most pleasurable moments as you watch the fruits of your labor grow. You may find that it will become like a hobby, where the temptation to destroy what you have built for some petty instant gratification will eventually fade. Be patient and you will eventually experience one of life's genuine pleasures, financial security.

As time passes, the investment environment may also change. Evaluate it continuously. Occasionally you may have to move your money from one vehicle to another. Your investment may no longer meet our minimum acceptable criteria over the long term, or you may find a better one.

You should also be cautious of rapidly rising or falling prices. They often signal an upcoming change in direction. Hence, if everybody is positive on the investment markets and prices are skyrocketing, it can be a signal to get out and take your profits because there is a major correction immediately ahead. After the correction you can jump back in at a discount and multiply your gains even more.

Likewise, after prices have fallen drastically, this may be the signal that a turnaround is imminent, signaling a time to buy. This is similar to contrarian investing, watching what the masses are doing and then doing the opposite since the masses are often wrong and are merely creating an artificial bubble by following what everyone else is doing. Bubbles don't continue forever, and knowing this can be tremendously profitable.

As with all investments, there are risks. Our job is to minimize these. One way is to wisely choose what investments you enter into in the first place. I will do this for you to the best of my abilities; however, if an investment goes sour because of unforeseen events, we must be prepared. This is the most difficult part because it involves discipline. We must be prepared to sell our investment before things get worse. Once a significant loss appears, things usually do get worse, and they rarely turn around. Here's why: By nature the markets are stacked against you. The problem is—and very few investors realize this—once you start losing money, the odds move against you at an ever-increasing pace the more you lose. That is, once you start losing money in a stock for example, it becomes ever more difficult to recoup your losses. There is a very specific explanation for this.

To illustrate, let's assume you just purchased $1,000 worth of IBM stock. If your stock's value increases to $1,500, you make a 50 percent profit. If it falls to $500 you make a 50 percent loss. Now here's the paradox: If you lose 50 percent of your money, to make back your money your stock has to appreciate by 100 percent—it has to double your loss ($500 worth of IBM stock has to appreciate by 100 percent in order for it to get back to the original $1,000). Therefore, in this scenario there is a 2:1 disadvantage. The greater the loss, the greater this disadvantage gets.

To minimize this disadvantage we set stop/loss orders. That is, we sell when our losses reach a predetermined amount, and this must be monitored closely. A 20 percent stop/loss order is conservative yet effective. If an investment reaches a 20 percent loss, we sell. Do not wait for a turnaround. Do not procrastinate, rationalize, or pretend. Sell immediately. The worst disasters have been the result of a lack of discipline in this area. If you cannot afford to lose 20 percent of your investment, you should never have entered into it in the first place. If you are upset at losing 20 percent of your money, you will be even more upset if you let your losses increase beyond 20 percent. Stick to your stop/loss with the utmost discipline. The best way to utilize stop/loss orders is to set them ahead of time with your broker so that they trigger automatically. We'll discuss stop/loss orders more later.

Finally, do not throw your money into anything—even my recommendations—you have not personally researched thoroughly. Remember that your quest for knowledge is an integral part of this plan. It will assure you that the investment decisions you make have a good risk-reward ratio. The key will be to conduct your own research to verify that any advice you get from me or anyone else is sound. Most of us are not experts in mutual funds, offshore funds, real estate, or any other investment vehicles. But there are plenty of people who are qualified.

Every wealthy person in the world has had help, advice, or a mentor from whom he or she has learned. Do the same—seek advice. The only question that qualifies as a stupid question is the one remaining unasked. Most people are willing to share their knowledge with you, so tap into this precious commodity. Napoleon Hill said, "The surest, fastest way to wealth is to follow in the footsteps of someone who has already done it." Another way to put this is that the only way to walk through a minefield is to walk in the footsteps of a person in front of you who is not covered in blood.

Before moving on to the next phase, let's play with some numbers to see what compounding, using 11 percent monthly compounded interest, can do for you. Here is a hypothetical model showing how the numbers work out given enough time. Let's assume an estate equal to that of an average American family.

Starting Capital:	$10,000.00
Total Monthly Income:	$3,000.00
Monthly savings (10%):	$300.00
Annual contribution:	$3,600.00

Income generated at 11% compounded interest:

Total capital after 10 years:	$95,587.68
Total Investment:	$46,000.00
Total capital after 20 years:	$351,422.07
Total Investment:	$82,000.00
Total capital after 30 years: $	1,116,149.33
Total Investment:	$118,000.00

Wow! After thirty years of saving just $300 per month, we can become millionaires if we compound at 11 percent interest. Our total investment was only one tenth of that amount. With compounding alone we can safely plan for our future. Better yet, with greater starting capital and greater monthly income, you'll generate even higher numbers than in our example—significantly higher.

Depending on your personal goals and your age, some people may not want to go any further than your compounded savings plan. It is conservative, safe (if researched and executed wisely), and very, very effective. It may be viewed as the perfect savings plan. If, however, you are anxious to accelerate your earnings and if you want more than just a passive means of wealth accumulation, then you must definitely read on.

Step #5: The next step is to move your money or a portion of your money into a leveraged investment such as real estate. The amount of time you leave your compounded investment to grow before moving into this next phase is ultimately up to you. You may choose to split your capital, leaving part of it in your savings plan indefinitely. Here are some guidelines to help you decide when to move some or all your money into real estate.

Depending on your financial situation, you must set a goal as to when you will move your investment into this next phase of our plan. The minimum recommended amount that you should have available to move is $20,000. It may be much higher for some people depending on their current means and total amount accumulated. Whatever the amount, this step can multiply the assets of rich and not-so-rich alike.

The following sample transaction will allow your capital to accelerate its appreciation beyond mere compounding. It is time to add leverage to your arsenal. Better yet, we will take advantage of a combination of leverage and compounding for truly wealth-building results.

It is important to note that there are always attractive real estate investments available. Even if the markets occasionally experience some dips, in the long term—and real estate is a long-term investment—profit is virtually guaranteed. They say, "You can never pay too much for real estate; you can only pay it too soon." Just have patience. Quality land is a very finite commodity. Unless we see a mass exodus to another planet, there is nothing that will change this.

To delve into real estate, getting a reasonable education by using books and a qualified broker will suffice. Just as thousands of Americans have made wise real estate investment decisions through thorough self-education, so can you. Keep in mind that there are more real estate millionaires in America than those resulting from any other endeavor. As advised earlier in this text, find qualified advice and then verify it.

The difference between the majority of real estate millionaires and you will be that you will know what was ultimately responsible for your fortune—compounding and leverage. Most real estate beneficiaries have no clue where their good fortune came from.

What you will be looking for is a property that has steady appreciation potential. Choosing a good neighborhood is probably the most important ingredient. As they say: location, location, location. If the property becomes your home, then you will also be sheltering yourself from temporary downturns in the market by simply substituting your rent payment with a mortgage payment. Home ownership should be considered an essential part of this plan. Making a fortune elsewhere does you no good if you are squandering it on rent payments.

In the following example you will see how leverage and compounding combine for an explosive effect. As before, we will use conservative assumptions and returns. Let's assume the following:

Start-up Capital	$20,000.00
Value of Property	$100,000.00
Leverage	80%
Amount Borrowed	$80,000.00
Conservative Annual Appreciation	6%
Value after 1 year	$106,000.00
Value after 10 years (compounded annually)	$179,085.00

Profit	$79,085.00
Return on Investment	395%
Average annual return	39.50%

Please note that your average annual return over ten years is 39.50 percent, despite the annual appreciation of the property being only 6 percent.

Is it any wonder that over half of all millionaires in America today made their fortunes in real estate? Most of them did not even know of their good fortune until it stared them in the face, and even then they did not know why it happened. You, on the other hand, armed with the right knowledge ahead of time, will be able to maximize your profit potential through careful planning.

Could we possibly ask for more? After ten years we have almost quadrupled our initial investment. If we were to continue enjoying the same appreciation for thirty years, the lifespan of most mortgages, the final value of the property would be $574,349. That's not bad considering we bought a $100,000 house with only $20,000 down. Furthermore, our monthly payments were not only a productive rent substitute but also largely tax deductible.

Please note that the actual appreciation could be significantly higher than I quoted in our example. History will confirm this. Real estate has always been one of the smartest investments anyone can make. If, on the other hand, disaster should strike and the property does not perform to our expectations, we have still built up equity with money that would otherwise have been thrown away as rent payments. This certainly satisfies our permanent safety requirements.

Step #6: Now that you have lots of equity, you're still driving a Chevy. Is there somewhere you went wrong? No, not unless you ignore the following advice.

When we move into real estate, it is vital to continue our savings and compounding exercises. We must continue to invest 10 percent of our income without interruption, but we are now doing it for a slightly different purpose. We are now saving to generate risk capital for ourselves. This capital allows us to raise our standard of living, not just our net worth as measured on paper.

Here is a snapshot of our current status:

We have purchased a property using the funds accumulated from our compounded savings plan. After we purchased the property, our deposits into our savings vehicle did not stop. We now have both a savings program and a property. The appreciation and increase in equity of the property are being fueled by the effects of inflation, supply and demand, and our monthly mortgage payments.

The savings that are continuing to accumulate can soon be used a little more liberally. Investments carrying slightly greater risk but promising a greater return are now acceptable. In the unlikely event of a total loss of our risk capital, we are not facing disaster. After all, our primary real estate investment is still appreciating untouched.

I recommend this strategy: As your compounding savings plan is again generating substantial amounts of money, use only your interest income for speculative investing. If for instance you buy a stock option for $500, you stand to make a sizable profit that could exceed 100 percent. Yet you could also lose the whole $500. If you use only your interest income from your savings, a total loss still means your principal remains unscathed. You have lost money you previously did not have. Therefore your savings cannot diminish because of an investment error. Furthermore, the net tax consequence is zero. The $500 was originally taxable interest income. If there is a complete loss of capital when investing this same $500, the tax write-off due to the loss will offset the taxable interest income. Obviously consult with your tax advisor on all matters regarding taxation.

The variety of investments to be considered with risk capital is virtually unlimited. From stocks and bonds to precious metals, there is a dizzying array of options (no pun intended). Use the knowledge you will have acquired since you started on the program. Make your choices. Set yourself reasonable parameters regarding safety versus risk, then have fun.

Step #7: It is at this point you may also consider the fourth key principle to multiplying money. I have not mentioned it so far because it is typically available only to high net worth individuals, and you need to have access to borrowed funds to implement it without using any of your own funds. But now you should have access to a loan by means of a second mortgage on your property. Furthermore, it is a variation of a principle already discussed—leverage. The difference is a striking one, however. With this variation you have total leverage. As mentioned, there are no funds of your own involved. That is, you are preparing to make maximum use of debt.

The following is the same principle that banks use to justify their existence. They lend for more than they borrow. You can do the same thing. If you borrow money at 8 percent interest and invest it somewhere else for a 10 percent return, you are making 2 percent on money that is not even yours. Basically you are making money from nothing. In the world of high finance, there is no better means of using your assets. Because you are not using any money of your own, you are receiving 100 percent leverage. This principle is similar to arbitrage, the simultaneous buying and selling of an asset, such as a currency, to take advantage of small price differences.

As mentioned, your ticket to this investment play is your property. Assuming your monthly payments have been made on time, you should typically have no problem getting a second mortgage or an equity line of credit. There are ways of applying this technique anywhere. You can, for instance, borrow money at 8 percent and invest it in your own business making more than 8 percent. It's the same principle.

Another example is discounted mortgages. Buying discounted mortgages offers an intriguing way to accomplish our goal and earn substantial spreads between what money costs you and what you can earn from it. Let's assume you find an ad in a newspaper selling a privately held $10,000 note (also called mortgage or trust deed) for $6,000. The seller is willing to give up their monthly income stream from payments in exchange for $6,000 immediate cash. They are discounting the note by $4,000, hence the term "discounted mortgages."

Assuming you purchase the note, if the monthly income from this note was $150, you will now receive those payments. Since your capital investment ($6,000) was substantially less than the original value of the note ($10,000), your percentage return on investment from the payments you receive will be proportionately higher. Annual returns of 25 percent are not uncommon.

Buying discounted mortgages can get rather complex, and one should research the mechanics carefully before investing, but the point is this: First, the note, just like a regular mortgage, is secured by property. The investment is therefore considered safer than most. Then, it can be bought with borrowed money. It follows that if you borrow from the equity in your home at 8 percent interest for example, reinvest the funds in the purchase of a discounted mortgage earning you over 20 percent, your income could be very handsome.

With a little research you will certainly be confronted with numerous investment choices that fit into this category. As mentioned, you may even consider using your borrowed funds to finance a business venture—yours or someone else's. Very exciting returns are possible.

Nonetheless, I am including this strategy only because it involves another financial principle, total leverage. This does not mean I am recommending it as a mandatory part of our plan. That is your choice.

Chapter 7:

Death and Taxes

Death and Taxes

---●---

"It's not what you earn that matters; it's what you keep."

Everyone knows that there are only two certainties in life, death and taxes. The best we can do regarding death is to delay it for as long as possible. Surprisingly the same is true with taxes.

The models and strategies we have examined are worth considerably less if we get taxed along the way, especially our compounded savings vehicles. If we pay taxes annually on our investments earned interest each year, then our effective income is reduced substantially.

Deferring taxation is our best and often our only defense. This means that you are taxed (on the entire profit) when you sell your investment regardless of how many years it took to accumulate this profit. With real estate this happens automatically but not with many dividend and interest income–generating investments. The best way to defer taxation that is available to everyone is your retirement plan. Monies held and invested within many types of retirement plans do not get taxed until those monies are withdrawn from the retirement plan.

When we redeem a tax-deferred investment and subsequently pay taxes on the entire profit, we are still faced with the pain of watching Uncle Sam inhale a good chunk of our earnings. The amount we are left with in the end is, however, substantially greater than if we get taxed along the way. By using the government's tax dollars to earn additional money that would not have been earned otherwise, we increase our total earnings.

Here is a striking example of the benefits of tax-deferred investing. Assume a $50,000 investment that compounds annually at 8 percent.

Principal investment $50,000
Compounded Interest Rate   8%

Year	Taxed Annually	Tax Deferred
5	$64,179.00	$73,466.00
10	$82,380.00	$107,946.00
15	$105,441.00	$158,608.00
20	$135,215.00	$233,048.00
25	$173,395.00	$342,423.00

You can see how much more money is available to contribute to the compounding effect when you defer taxation. This is the money that you would have otherwise had to pay in taxes each year. By deferring taxation, you are able to use those tax dollars to earn more dollars. The end result speaks for itself.

The concept of tax-deferred investing is included here as it becomes an integral part of the chapter on where and how to realize adequate compounded returns. It makes sense to understand the concept of deferred taxation beforehand.

Chapter 8:

Not Just Money

Not Just Money

The tools are now at your disposal. It is up to you to apply them in a fashion suitable to your goals and present lifestyle. Remember that the most important aspect of everything you have read so far is simply the importance of having the right knowledge. This refers to knowledge on how money behaves and how it accumulates.

This book represents the first quantum leap forward in providing you with the knowledge you need to grow rich. What remains for you to learn is the information you need to gather BEFORE you invest. These are specifics that have to do with the many individual investment vehicles available to you in the current investment climate as investment conditions typically change slightly from year to year.

Even if you never invest in the manner described, you will still have a much better appreciation of how money can be put to work effectively. You will understand the power of saving correctly and regularly, and you will have the knowledge that you can create wealth in the same way that others have created it for themselves. This knowledge can provide you with a new frame of reference that will enrich your life and, if you choose to do so, even guide you effortlessly into a higher standard of living. At the very least you will no longer have to wonder how so many people can afford a $120,000 Mercedes while you cannot.

If you remember only one thing from this whole text, remember this:

The principles of money have extraordinary applications that go far beyond the financial examples cited in this book. In almost any method of wealth creation, somewhere hidden inside is saving correctly, compounding your earnings, leveraging your assets, or investing for more than your cost of capital.

To illustrate how any of the four principles cited can affect our lives without involving money or investments, let's examine some of them in more detail.

First, let's examine leverage—probably the single-most effective tool that a manager, executive, or entrepreneur has to accelerate the production and growth of their business. By managing through people, they use leverage via the skilled use of delegation. One person can do only so much, but it is the individual recognizing this limitation who has the edge. By mobilizing others to do tasks that work toward a common goal, the manager leverages his or her abilities and knowledge. He provides the input in the form of informed instructions, motivation, and reward, whereas his numerous workers provide the output. The output can be vastly greater than the manager could have ever achieved by himself without leveraging his abilities through other people.

To further illustrate this point, imagine an entrepreneur who currently operates a successful business. He wants to open another company but does not have the time. Thus, he trains someone to do it for him, leveraging his abilities by introducing the same know-how to someone else, effectively duplicating himself. If he limits his direct involvement to only financing and guidance, he can do this with as many companies as he wishes. Alone, he could probably never effectively operate more than one or possibly two ventures. By leveraging his knowledge via skilled delegation, the entrepreneur can have more companies operating for his benefit.

The entrepreneur may also teach the executives in each of his companies to delegate in the same fashion, showing them how to duplicate what they have been taught into another level of workers. He will then be leveraging his abilities and compounding his output, thereby using two of our principles.

The same two principles, compounding and leverage, are at work in multilevel marketing. Each participant leverages him or herself by introducing new members into their "downline" organization, consequently earning commissions on their sales also. Compounding is achieved by allowing this sales force to recruit and train their own organizations, who in turn do the same, and they in turn do the same again, etc. This happens through as many levels as the company's compensation plan allows for, sometimes without any limitation—that is, through infinity. The network marketer will earn commissions from all their sales as well.

By using leverage and compounding, the network marketer effectively creates a family-tree effect that grows wider and wider at lower levels. In the end a single marketer can have thousands of individuals in his or her organization, all working toward his financial benefit. The earnings potential is staggering.

Multilevel marketing has to its credit more millionaires than any endeavor other than real estate. Amway, Shaklee, Avon, Nikken, and dozens of other companies have used their multilevel structure to achieve what conventional means could never do. Some companies even grew so fast it drove them out of business. It seems they lost the means to support the huge organizations they had created. Their growth rate increased exponentially at a rate that was simply unsustainable.

Franchising is another ingenious way to use leverage to expand the earnings potential of certain companies. By allowing individual operators to influence their destinies, McDonald's, Burger King, Subway, Howard Johnson Hotels, and other firms have propelled themselves into economic powerhouses controlling thousands of locations. We can see their offspring in almost any mall in America and across the globe.

An unfortunate by-product of this is that all malls are starting to look alike. We see the same franchises everywhere we go. In fact, many of these phenomena are exerting their influence internationally as well. It is not hard to find a Pizza Hut restaurant, McDonald's, or a Marriott Hotel in most parts of the world, now even in Russia and China. Without the skilled use of franchising, delegation, and leverage, these companies would probably still be unknown to most of us.

Another common application of leverage is in direct-mail advertising. Ask yourself how many people would buy a very hot product from you if you had to sell it in person? Even with the use of conference halls, your face-to-face sales exposure is limited. With mail order your exposure is limited only by your imagination and the amount of money you have available for postage and printing. You can mail the same sales literature to thousands, even millions of people simultaneously, resulting in a highly leveraged use of your message. Television and print advertising incorporate the same leveraging effect.

In the nonbusiness world we leverage our talents, our acquaintances, and our knowledge. Wealth ultimately flows to those who know how to use this information and to those who recognize the far-reaching applications that these principles have in all aspects of their lives.

Paul Zane Pilzer suggests in his book *Unlimited Wealth* that the ultimate form of leverage is technology. He notes, "Technology today is what makes one individual's earning power one thousand times that of another."

With the widespread use of computers, we are seeing a "multiplier effect" take place in all areas of research and study. Because of the computer's awesome speed, storage capacity, and computing power, it takes less time to complete tasks and distribute information. This in turn accelerates the development of new technologies and ideas.

Technology has a multiplier effect on itself as each new technological advance becomes the foundation for another advance. This has been the foundation of man's advancement since the beginning of recorded time, literally. Between the years 1500 and 1750 AD the volume of knowledge humanity had acquired since the start of recorded history until that point doubled. By 1900 it doubled again, then again by 1950, and again by 1965. We can see that what at first took 250 years to achieve, then took only 150 years, then only fifty, then only fifteen. The time it takes for us to double the amount of information available to us keeps getting shorter and shorter. At this rate, by the year 2020, the volume of information recorded and available to us will double every three days.

The Internet has been an incredible quantum leap forward and is now accessible to anyone with a PC. The Internet is the largest computer network in the world. It is actually thousands of smaller networks linked together. When previous Vice President Al Gore spoke of the "information superhighway," he didn't realize that it was already here. Nonetheless, his speech accelerated interest in the Internet to such a degree that it went from complete obscurity outside universities, government agencies, and computer experts, to almost a household word within a single year.

Anyone with an Internet connection can be a publisher— a mass distributor of knowledge, information and misinformation, fact, fancy, and fiction. Never before in history have so many people been able to communicate so much to so many. New information, better information, faster information, and even more information—these are the components of modern-day leverage.

Like leverage, the power of compounding can also affect our lives most profoundly without involving money or investments. The following example is quite different from the preceding ones in that it represents a problem instead of an opportunity. In fact, it represents a problem of monolithic proportions. Compounding, in this instance, will eventually result in our own extinction if we do not learn to harness its ferocious power. I am referring to compounding as it relates to population growth.

With over six billion people occupying our planet, it is common knowledge that our world is already overpopulated. What is foreign to most of us, however, is the severity of the problem.

Let's start with a simple thesis: Since our environment, the Earth, and the universe, are finite in size, all growth must eventually cease. "But the universe is pretty big," you say. Not quite. Enter compounding.

At a 1 percent per annum growth rate, something doubles in quantity every seventy-two years. Therefore, if we now have six billion people on planet Earth, in seventy-two years it will be twelve billion, in another seventy-two years it will be twenty-four billion. At that rate of doubling (every seventy-two years), we do not have more than a few hundred years of uncontrolled growth left before we deplete our environment and annihilate ourselves. This is especially true since our actual growth rate is nearly double that of our example. It is actually about 1.8 percent per annum, which means our population is doubling approximately every forty years.

Here's another sobering scenario: even if there were only 100 people on Earth right now, after the population doubles 512 times, which would take a little over 36,000 years, at only a 1 percent annual growth rate, the number of people would exceed the number of subatomic particles in the entire universe. Granted, 36,000 years seems like a long time, but let's not look at this only as it relates to our own lifetime. Even thinking in terms of hundreds, thousands, or even tens of thousands of years, these are all completely insignificant lengths of time when compared to the future or history of our planet.

The Earth is projected to exist for another five or six billion years before the sun expands and destroys all the planets, including our Earth. That's a very long time compared to the history of humanity, measured in mere thousands of years. Even the dinosaurs existed for forty million years. Yet at our current rate of population growth, we will self-destruct within the next few hundred years. In the process, our arrogance will likely cause us to doom most species of life to the same fate.

Without any further acceleration of our growth rate, we are already at a critical point. We must realize that population growth must not merely decrease, it must cease altogether and it must do so now.

The above examples are not just theoretical. Professor Isaac Asimov has shown that if population growth were to continue at the present rate for another 1,800 years, the mass of humanity will exceed the mass of the Earth. After only 5,500 years, the mass of humanity would exceed the mass of the entire universe. Clearly this is impossible. Population growth will stop long before this eventuality. The question becomes: how will it stop? Will we be able to curb population explosion, or will nature do it for us, as in a cataclysmic event such as our own mass extinction?

You may think you see the heavens as our savior, but colonizing other planets would only delay the inevitable by an equally insignificant period, a few hundred years at best. The same holds true if a global catastrophe such as Ebola wiped out 90 percent of our population. Doomsday would be delayed by only about 250 years, the time it takes for us to get back to our current population. You see, if 90 percent of our population suddenly disappeared, doubling the remaining 10 percent (10%, 20%, 40%, 80%, 160% ...) every seventy-two years would require only slightly more than three doublings before we arrive back at the original 100 percent, equating to about 250 years. *Hence we see that even a 1 percent annual growth rate in population is a guaranteed recipe for extinction within a few hundred years.*

The power of compounded growth is overwhelming. Nothing short of a complete restructuring of our society can stand in its way. We must rethink our views toward abortion, birth control (voluntary and mandatory), euthanasia, the developing world, and how we use our economic resources.

Essentially we must redefine what we consider to be moral. Our current definition is obsolete. If it is not revised, it will kill us in the name of virtuousness.

Do we use our resources to give foreign aid to developing countries like Kenya, which has a staggering 4 percent growth rate (their population doubles every eighteen years), or do we use those same funds to finance new educational facilities in this country? Do we provide subsidized health care to five million illegal aliens, or do we use the money to reduce a deficit that will leave us all without benefits if left to grow much farther? Tough choices have to be made; our survival depends on it.

To add to the misery, economic growth is limited in exactly the same way as population growth, also due to the compounding effect. Take our budget, for example. Every year the US budget, be it for military or health-care spending, is automatically allowed to grow by an amount that is supposedly justified by increasing costs. What is ignored however, is that growth spending is silently compounding at the same time. If, for instance, the growth allowance is 5 percent this year, we will grow our expenditures to 105 percent of the original. Next year it will be another 5 percent, but not on top of the original 100 percent; it will be 5 percent of the new 105 percent.

As this continues indefinitely, the actual percentage increase is almost irrelevant. It is the fact that we are compounding our expenditure increases that will drive this country out of business. Compounding at any rate is suicide in our current economic plight. Total expenditures must decrease; a merely symbolic decrease in the rate of increase is just not sufficient.

It is ironic that we are about to enter an era where compounding will likely be used to solve the problems caused by compounding in the first place. Our budget deficit is now so large that our government is unable to reduce it without making us all suffer. At this point even massive spending cuts would hurt almost as much as they would help.

There is a way out, however. The solution is the compounding effect of inflation. By inflating the money supply, we create a cheaper dollar. That is, we will aim for a dollar worth about half its present value or purchasing power.

Here's the rationale: If the rate of inflation is 10 percent per year, it will take only seven years for the dollar to lose half its value. This also means that our deficit will lose half its value. We will cheat our way out of our obligations. The number of dollars we pay back will be the full amount of our debt, but each dollar will be worth only half as much.

Our deficit could be substantially reduced in less than a decade, and Uncle Sam need not even ask our permission. All we need to do is turn on the printing presses. It would be completely covert. Hence I predict this will be our administration's medicine of choice. The cost to us will be tremendous, yet most will not realize it for many years.

Inflation, the result of Central Bank money creation, can solve our $18 trillion debt problem, albeit at great expense to us. As a by-product, your personal taxes will increase without your knowledge! You see, inflation actually causes your income to rise, or so it seems. In real value you will not be making any more since the dollar will be worth less—you'll be lucky to break even. You will, however, move into higher tax brackets, increasing your percentage of income tax paid.

Compounding, as with population growth, places rapidly approaching limits on economic growth. Our economies cannot continue to grow at any rate without interruption because our natural resources are limited. Since they are ultimately the source of all economic expansion, we will run out of them in no time at all. If we suddenly ran out of crude oil, for example (and eventually we will), every economy on Earth will grind to a halt because a comparable substitute is not fully in place yet. How much oil do we have left, fifty to one hundred years' worth?

The clock is ticking. Because of compounding, it ticks faster and faster. Unfortunately, knowing mankind's current oblivion to this problem, we run the real risk of not waking up until it is too late, and that is sooner than we realize. There can be only one solution if we want to improve or at least maintain our standard of living, save our environment, reduce the risk of war, and eliminate famine—our population must decrease!

It is interesting that the wealthiest and most educated countries, or even the wealthiest and most educated families, have the lowest birthrate. As education leads to wealth, wealth leads to lower birthrates, and lower birthrates can help to ensure our survival. Draw your own conclusions.

On a lighter note, gambling is another unlikely place where the compounding principle can be found. Once again, its application can produce both opportunity and pitfall.

Among seasoned gamblers it is widely known that there is a very simple technique that comes closest to a guarantee of winning at almost any game, from roulette and craps to blackjack and poker. It is the doubling principle applied to your bets.

Let's assume you're playing roulette and you make a one-dollar bet on black. That means that if a black number comes up, you'll double your money. If a red number comes up, you lose.

Here's what you do: If you lose, double your bet the next time around. If you lose again, double your bet again. Keep this up until you win. Since the odds of winning or losing are very close to 50:50, it is highly probable that sooner or later you'll win, probably sooner rather than later. When you do win, you'll win back all the money you lost, plus one dollar (or whatever the amount of your first bet was). Then you would start the process over again until you win your next dollar. (Of course, you can do this starting with ten dollars, a hundred dollars, or any other amount.) In compounding terms, you are compounding your bet 100 percent every time you lose, from one dollar to two dollars, to four, to eight, to sixteen, to thirty-two, etc.

The technique is almost guaranteed. The key word is "almost." First of all, casinos know this trick, and they keep a watchful eye out, but there's an even more ominous trap. Due to the compounding growth effect (see the thirty-day doubling example in the chapter titled "Sit Back, Relax, Get Rich"), if you hit an unlucky streak, you need very substantial cash flow to keep up with the ever-increasing bet requirements until you win. Say you lose ten times in a row—your next bet has to be $1,024 just to keep going. If you lose again, your next bet is $2,048 to stay in the game. Even if you could keep this up for a while, is it worth it for a payoff of only one dollar? Nonetheless, you are seeing the compounding effect at work.

Finally, let me explain my favorite use of the compounding principle. I call it brain compounding, and it makes all my recommendations for increasing your level of knowledge that much more relevant. It works like this: When you go out and learn something new, that new piece of knowledge becomes a new tool in your arsenal of brain power, knowledge, and decision-making abilities. That new piece of knowledge can now be used to acquire another new piece of knowledge, possibly more profound or complex than the one responsible for acquiring this one.

In essence, the smarter you become by acquiring more and more knowledge, the more that knowledge can help you become even smarter, and this happens at an ever-increasing rate. Learn something new, and then use what you've learned on top of what you already know to learn something else that would have been unavailable to you without your newfound baseline of knowledge. To again use the analogy from the book *The Richest Man in Babylon*, each new piece of knowledge can become a worker who can earn you more knowledge, which in turn can do the same. Now that's compounding at its best!

Look around you. You'll find the principles of wealth in the most unlikely places. As mentioned before, the principles of wealth are natural laws. Mankind did not invent them. Our job is to humbly recognize their power and influence over all aspects of our lives and hopefully learn to harness them for our own predetermined benefit.

Chapter 9:

Applying the Secrets of Wealth

Applying the Secrets of Wealth

The principles outlined in this text are genuinely responsible for the vast majority of wealthy individuals—yesterday and today. Now that these principles are no longer secrets, they are yours to use also.

You can apply the principles in several ways. First, you can follow the plan in this book. It will work. All you need to do is adapt it to your financial condition, goals, and the current investment climate. You should, however, also apply the principles to any endeavors you may already be planning or any you may be currently involved in. This may be your business, your investments, or any other financial venture. The principles of wealth will enable you to supercharge your financial machine until your efforts generate truly wealth-building results. You will not work harder, but you will work smarter.

The first step is to examine if the venture you have or the one you are considering already contains one or more of our principles. Here's how you do this: Let's assume it's a business. The following examination determines whether your business needs a shot in the arm or whether the one you may be considering has true potential. Conversely, a quick analysis will also determine those that may be a waste of time. The difference is the opportunity to get rich versus being able to make a mere living at best.

The prime ingredients to look for are compounding, leverage, and debt (investing borrowed funds for more than the cost of those funds), all of which can take on many different disguises. Here are some examples:

1) Buying a Franchise – Assume you are reviewing the possibility of buying a franchise. It can be anything from vinyl repair to a McDonald's restaurant. You have several options:

    a. You can buy a franchise with cash and manage it for income. This is the least favorable choice because you are spending your money and your time to earn a living. The only advantage is you will be quasi-independent, but even that is debatable because of the long hours required.

    b. You can buy a franchise with borrowed money and let someone manage it for you, which is much better. Obviously you will want to spend some time doing hands-on managing, but your time will eventually be spent more productively elsewhere.

c. You can do everything outlined in "b," and then do it again with another franchise, then again and again.

Option "c" has the greatest potential of all. In each scenario the total time you spend working remains similar, but the amount of personal savings you invest diminishes when you finance, and each scenario shows an ever-increasing usage of the principles we have outlined. This enables you to have more locations, effectively multiplying the amount of money you can make by the number of locations you control. You are thus leveraging your time and your resources. Your return on investment depends only on how far you want to extend this particular means of leveraging your resources. You can have three locations or three hundred. It is entirely up to you.

2) Owning Your Own Business – In this example, assume you already have a small business selling natural cosmetics (or anything else). Your company sells to health-food stores via a small direct sales force. Already you have introduced some leverage into your business by allowing additional salespeople to help open and service accounts because you can do only so much by yourself.

Your business is doing quite well and growing slowly but steadily. If it continues at the current pace and a more aggressive competitor does not steal your market, or a recession does not dwindle your sales to the point of insolvency, you may pass on a lucrative little venture to your kids one day. But will you be sunning yourself in Bermuda? Probably not.

Here's what may come to mind after reading *The Secrets of Wealth*. First, borrow money to expand. You'll be investing the money for more than it is costing you (one of our principles), and the cost can be well worth it. Even though you will add the burden of interest expense to your balance sheet, your increased pool of capital should earn more than your cost of those same funds. Revenues and profits can soar. If your interest expense decreases your percentage of net income somewhat, that's okay because the dollar amount will nonetheless increase. As they say, 1 percent of a billion is still ten million.

Next, leverage your advertising. Learn the methods of direct mail, display, social media, and word-of-mouth advertising. You can reach thousands more people, even millions, by making your message heard louder and farther. The payoff can be enormous.

Leverage your sales force also. Make them distributors who will be more productive for you if they are operating their own little businesses. Employees will produce a maximum of only eight hours' worth of work in a day. A smart distributor/entrepreneur can give you a hundred hours' worth of productivity each day if they are also allowed, for example, to recruit additional people to do more selling.

Finally, use your earnings wisely. Ten percent of your profit should immediately go into a compounding investment. This may be even a further business expansion vehicle that will enable you to earn more dollars from the dollars you have already earned. As mentioned, the principles of wealth—in this case saving 10 percent and compounding—can take on different disguises. Be creative in your applications.

If you place part of the earnings from your business into an investment, treat it as you would your personal savings plan. It will be there for you on a rainy day so that you may eventually enjoy that sunny day in Bermuda. As with your personal savings plan, do not dip into your investment. Allow the power of compounding your interest to work its magic.

3) Real Estate – If you own property, you can do some of the same things described above. A property can be treated just like a business. You can borrow against it and then buy more property with the proceeds. Borrow against the new property, buy more, etc. If you allow the rental income from each property to make the respective mortgage payment, you can carry this on forever.

If you want your net worth to exceed a million dollars one day, follow this advice: save 10 percent of your income, invest it for an acceptable compounded return, then buy a dozen properties by borrowing against one to finance the next. You will be using all four principles of wealth.

Donald Trump used this method of compounding a leveraged real estate investment until he controlled hundreds of millions of dollars in real estate. Obviously don't spread yourself as thin as he did by over-borrowing. Otherwise the slightest downturn in the real estate market will put you on your bank's "Most Wanted" list. You see, periodic declines in value are a fact of life when owning real estate. The beauty of investing in real estate is, however, that these declines are almost always temporary. This simply means that your portfolio needs to be able to weather an occasional storm during periods of decline.

Nonetheless, one has to admit that Donald Trump deserves tremendous recognition. Even when his credit rating dipped to new lows, he never lost the power of leverage. This is a beautiful example of leveraging your debt—but it's not necessarily a recommended strategy. You see, Donald Trump used his fall to his advantage because he owed so much money to his banking creditors. This is because when you owe a million dollars to your bank, your bank owns you. But when you owe a hundred million dollars to your bank, you own them. That's leverage!

4) Network Marketing – In this final example let's assume you are evaluating a business opportunity such as a network marketing distributorship.

Network marketing or multilevel marketing works like this: By becoming a distributor for a network marketing company, you are obtaining the right to recruit or sponsor new distributors into the company. Every time you sell the company's product to friends, family, or whomever, you receive a commission for your efforts. As you bring other people into the program, you will be paid commissions on their sales as well. If they in turn also recruit distributors, you will be paid on their sales as well. This can happen on several more levels, depending on the company's compensation plan.

The potential to be paid commissions on other people's sales, and on the sales of their recruits, is very enticing. Few people actually realize how potent this type of plan really is. Any loyal student of *The Secrets of Wealth* will recognize leverage and compounding being applied in a manner that would be hard to surpass anywhere else.

Most network marketing companies provide the following simplified example to describe how their method of marketing has become responsible for a $40 billion worldwide industry. If you recruit five people who in turn recruit five people each, and this happens again with each level of recruits, you will create a family-tree effect that rapidly expands as you reach lower levels. Here are the actual numbers:

Level 1	You sponsor 5 people	5
Level 2	They in turn sponsor 5 people (5x5)	25
Level 3	They each sponsor 5 people (25x5)	125
Level 4	They each sponsor 5 people (125x5)	625
Level 5	They each sponsor 5 people (625x5)	3,125
Level 6	They each sponsor 5 people (3,125x5)	15,625
Total number of people sponsored		19,530

Isn't that incredible? Through the process of duplicating your own efforts, you have effectively amassed a "downline" of almost 20,000 people selling your products or services. And all you did was recruit five people and then taught them to do the same. If the company pays you monthly commissions on the sales of 20,000 people—that is, on six levels—it doesn't take a scientist to recognize the awesome opportunity you have just uncovered.

Obviously you must check out a company's offerings, including their compensation plan, because some, as mentioned in a previous chapter, collapse as a result of their own phenomenal growth rate. However, from a marketing standpoint, you are looking at what may be the ultimate application of two principles of wealth, leverage and compounding, without the occasional sleepless nights associated with debt.

Anyone who fully understands why network marketing is so effective will correctly determine how to best utilize their time and effort. That is, anything that encourages geometric growth or the multiplier effect such as training, recruiting, and motivating one's downline distributors should receive continuous attention.

Some of my shrewdest readers may recognize that there is an even more potent application of the principles of wealth than the previous example, which has not yet been discussed. What if network marketing were applied to a leveraged investment such as real estate or commodities futures? A leveraged investment would then be leveraged again. It has been tried, both in real estate and in gold futures. If you come across such an opportunity, I advise extreme caution. It is simply too much of a good thing, and failures have been the norm. Furthermore, because the consumer is being placed at substantial risk, the legal challenges these companies face can be daunting. An overleveraged empire such as this simply doesn't inspire a sense of stability over the long term.

The previous four examples, in addition to the chapter titled "Not Just Money," serve to show you that the principles of wealth are all around us. They always have been, and they always will be. They are at the root of many problems, such as exponential population growth, and they are responsible for many opportunities, such as leveraged real estate. The principles of wealth can work in both directions within the same phenomenon, such as with commodities futures, creating either staggering profits or total ruin. They can be found almost anywhere—in the financial world, technology, our minds, or in nature. One thing stands out though: the principles of wealth can be harnessed, manipulated, and controlled for our benefit. But first, we must recognize them and their widespread applications. Hence this book.

Your goal should be to integrate the principles of wealth into your thinking until you recognize their presence in areas that previously may have seemed unlikely. Here's another consideration: In the previous four examples, you will notice a gradual increase in the number of principles that apply as you move from one example to the next. You will also notice an increasingly efficient use of those principles. But what else is being introduced? Time.

You are making more efficient use of your time when you introduce the principles of wealth. You are not working more, but you are working smarter. This means that you are not working five times as much, but you are doing five times the amount of work in the same amount of time. Working smarter means leveraging your time. As mentioned before, it is how we spend our time that determines our level of success, nothing else. Hence the most important application of one of the principles of wealth, leverage, is found in how we use the time available to us.

If you still cannot see a way to incorporate *The Secrets of Wealth* into your activities, recognize that you have available to you the greatest tool known to man. That tool is your own creativity. To be creative means only one thing—you make it up! You can literally invent new and different ways of applying the principles in this book. A new application is an invention. You are capable of inventing. Inventing is creating. Creating is imagining. Imagining is making it up. Making it up is nothing more than solving a problem, and every problem has a solution. If you look hard enough, you'll find it. This is not rhetorical gibberish. America is the land of opportunity because you can literally create your own job here. Where there was no job or opportunity previously, it is entirely possible for you to create one. To paraphrase Paul Zane Pilzer and his definition of wealth, "It is no longer finding a need and filling it; it is imagining a need and creating it." The only thing that can cause you to fail is not trying hard enough, not trying long enough, or worse, not trying at all.

Chapter 10:

Where To, When To, and How To

Where To, When To, and How To

————————————•◦•————————————

This is definitely the most difficult chapter to provide you as this is not about the timeless principles themselves but rather where to apply the timeless principle of compounding in today's investment climate for an acceptable and secure return.

The principles of wealth we have explored have always been there and will continue to be there unchanged. That's why I refer to them as timeless. Finding the right place to apply them in today's financial markets is an entirely different matter. Those details will always change over time as the economy and the markets change, although my recommendations should remain relevant for the foreseeable future. Nonetheless, once again, I strongly urge you to investigate any investment yourself so that you know it is still right for the time you decide to get into it.

Today's investment climate is not ideal considering how low interest rates have sunk. This does not mean, however, that there are no investments available to us with an acceptable rate of return while still maintaining adequate levels of stability and safety. We just have to look a little harder. In fact, there is a way for you to get compounded returns that can far exceed any returns available in the current investment and interest-rate climate: use the proceeds from a leveraged investment— reinvest those proceeds into a new leveraged investment, thereby compounding your earnings, and later reinvest it all in another leveraged investment, and then repeat the process. Compounded returns of any magnitude are theoretically possible. Here is a chart to show you how lucrative this strategy can be, even at rates of return that are not stratospheric.

Years	15%	25%	30%
1	$11,500	$12,500	$13,000
2	$13,225	$15,625	$16,900
3	$15,208	$19,531	$21,970
4	$17,490	$24,414	$28,561
5	$20,113	$30,517	$37,129
6	$23,130	$38,146	$48,268
7	$26,600	$47,683	$62,748
8	$30,590	$59,604	$81,573
9	$35,178	$74,505	$106,044
10	$40,455	$93,132	$137,858
11	$46,523	$116,415	$179,211
12	$53,502	$145,519	$232,980
13	$61,527	$181,898	$302,875
14	$70,757	$227,373	$393,737
15	$81,370	$284,217	$511,858
16	$93,576	$355,271	$665,416
17	$107,612	$444,089	$865,041
18	$123,754	$555,111	$1,124,554
19	$142,317	$693,889	$1,461,920
20	$163,665	$867,361	$1,900,496
21	$188,215	$1,084,202	$2,470,645
22	$216,447	$1,355,252	$3,211,838
23	$248,914	$1,694,065	$4,174,390
24	$286,251	$2,117,582	$5,428,007
25	$329,189	$2,646,977	$7,056,409

Huge compounded returns are possible by using leverage to make a large return, then reinvesting it all to compound into a new leveraged investment, and repeating the process as often as you like.

You have learned how the principles of wealth can be applied in a number of different areas including real estate, your business, franchising, network marketing, etc. But when it comes to compounding your interest, most people want to look at our financial markets to create a somewhat passive source of income. That is what this chapter is about. Much of what we will discuss will involve the option of investing within your retirement plan in order to defer taxation for a substantially greater end result as described in the chapter "Death and Taxes."

If any of my recommendations become invalid, then our financial system will have morphed substantially and this is not entirely foreseeable. If such an unlikely transformation of our financial system should occur, it doesn't mean you will not be able to find similar returns elsewhere. You will just have to investigate where our principles are best applied in those current financial markets. Notice how "invest" is part of the word "investigate."

For clarity, this chapter will be divided into the following subheadings:

- Retirement Accounts

- What Not To Invest In

- Index Funds

- Annuities

- Dividend Stocks

- Whole Life Insurance

- Protecting Against Declines

Retirement Accounts

A retirement account is not an investment. A retirement account is an investment vehicle. This means that a retirement account is like a holding account for your money until you reach retirement age. Within that vehicle or holding account your money is directed into certain investments either by yourself or by someone assigned with the task, depending on the type of retirement account, self-directed or otherwise.

401(k)s and IRAs have a specific advantage that makes them strategically very important to your future level of prosperity and therefore to this plan.

First of all, the money you put into a retirement account is tax deductible. But more importantly, retirement accounts allow you to defer taxation until you withdraw funds. This means that money you would normally be paying out in taxes right now can work for you to create more money from interest or appreciation. That means you are making money from money that is not technically yours. It belongs to the government. However, the government is allowing you to hold on to it and use it until you withdraw it during your retirement years. Using the government's money to earn money is especially valuable when your income compounds.

Deferring your tax obligations until retirement creates a dramatic positive effect on the accumulation of your nest egg. For this reason you want to maximize your contributions every year. Your CPA will help explain your contribution limits to you, depending on which type of retirement account you have or are eligible for.

Retirement accounts do have one dilemma that some shrewd thinkers may be anticipating as they read this. It has to do with the level of taxation at the time of withdrawal. If you are going to be taxed many years from now instead of today, what guarantees you that tax rates won't be substantially higher than today's rates? Actually, considering the current financial situation the entire world is in, it is a virtual guarantee that tax rates will go up. For this reason it would be financially advantageous to be taxed now, at lower rates and on a smaller amount of money, than later when tax rates are higher and you've accumulated a lot of money.

The option that allows you to pay your taxes now on the amount you put into your retirement account is called ROTH. You can have a ROTH IRA or a ROTH 401(k). The great part is that when you put money into a ROTH and pay your taxes on that money right away, any future earnings are completely tax-free, both on appreciation and on withdrawals.

Let me give you an example to illustrate my point. Let's assume your current tax rate is 30 percent, and years from now when you retire everyone's tax rates will have gone up and yours is 40 percent. Wouldn't it seem wiser to pay 30 percent taxes on your contributions right now rather than paying 40 percent on all the contributions and growth years from now? This is especially true when you consider that today you may be paying taxes only on your contributions, say $10,000, whereas when you retire, you'd be paying taxes on your original contributions PLUS its appreciation. Depending on how many years your plan has had to grow, this could be double, triple, or more than what you originally contributed.

For the purposes of this wealth-building plan, a highly desirable option is to find a compounded investment within a ROTH retirement plan. You will pay your taxes now but never pay taxes on that money again, regardless of how much it grows. Knowing that tax rates will likely go up, this way you will end up with a lot more money later.

One thing to remember is that your retirement account is only as good as what's in it. We will discuss some investments to consider for your ROTH retirement plan, but first let's review some investments to avoid at all costs.

What Not To Invest In

Two words: mutual funds.

Mutual funds are one of the most popular investments out there, yet they are also the biggest Wall Street rip-off ever invented, bilking the average investor out of the majority of what should have been the investor's returns—and they don't even know it. It is basically a skimming operation. The problem is with fees that you don't know about because they're buried in the fine print.

Let's start with performance. The $13 trillion mutual fund industry doesn't do nearly as well as they advertise, with 96 percent of them failing to beat the market over any reasonable period of time. What happened to these people being so-called experts?

Consistency is the first issue. A fund that does well one year rarely does well a few years later. Their performance bounces all over the place. Therefore, the frequently heard disclosure "Past performance is no indicator of future profits" is truer than people realize, mostly because of misleading advertising on the part of the entire mutual fund industry. Just as statistics can be skewed to make pretty much any case you want, performance charts for mutual funds are manipulated to show you only periods of growth, cleverly giving you the impression of long-term positive performance.

The mutual fund industry's greatest skill is not in performance but in masterfully hiding a plethora of fees unknown to all but the industry itself, and this includes no-load funds. Fees typically add up to over 3 percent, which could be half or more of the mutual fund's profit. And that's not a one-time fee—that's every year!

If you take the time to read the dozens of pages of fine print, you will find fee after fee, cleverly hidden and disguised. This means that the returns advertised by mutual funds are not the returns earned by you, the investor in those same funds. In fact, over time, up to 70 percent of your entire basket of mutual fund's earnings and appreciation could eventually be lost to fees. According to Tony Robbins' fabulously detailed analysis of this dilemma in his book *Money: Master the Game*, this can add up to ten to thirty times what it should cost. Maybe this is why almost half of all fund managers do not own a single share of the fund that they manage. Although Tony Robbins' book is over 600 pages of small print and therefore not an easy read, I still consider it the best revelation of this scam published to date. I highly recommend you pick up a copy.

The biggest drain on your profits is revenue-sharing fees, also known as pay-to-play fees. This simply means that a significant portion of your profits will be subtracted as a cleverly hidden fee. And the amount they take for only this fee? A staggering 20 percent of your profits.

Here's an example taken from a newsletter called The Crux to illustrate how damaging mutual-fund fees can be to your retirement nest egg. Let's consider an investor who puts $5,000 into his retirement plan per year. Let's further assume that the mutual funds he invests in earn 8 percent annually, and he pays a 2 percent annual fee. Over forty years he accumulates $786,000. If the fee had been a much more reasonable 1 percent, he would have ended up with $1,045,000. That's an additional $259,000! Now consider that most mutual funds charge in excess of 2 percent. Fortunately there are ways to reduce your fees to less than 1 percent. These two variables would make our example even more extreme.

So where do we go to get an acceptable return with reasonable fees of 1 percent or less? The answer is index funds acquired from the right source. This is what we will explore next.

Index Funds

Why is it that we always hear about traders and fund managers trying to beat the market? The reason is that the market as a whole is difficult to beat. Although America's stock market performance is cyclical (i.e., alternating up and down), almost every time it goes up, it moves to new highs. The market typically does better than all but a small minority of traders or their mutual funds. And after all those horrendous mutual fund fees are deducted from your account every year, the pack that outperforms the market at the bottom line is even smaller.

An index fund is a basket of stocks. The S&P 500 is one of the most well known. It tracks or mimics the performance of the top 500 companies (ranked by market capitalization) as a group. Standard & Poor's does the analysis and selects which stocks belong in their index. Most of these companies are very well known because of their size (e.g., Apple, Amazon, and Exxon).

We track the market's performance by looking at index funds. They are the ones we hear about on the news and on business programs. An index fund tracks a large portion of the market, but not just stocks. Index funds can also track bonds, real estate, or commodities such as precious metals. Nonetheless, the most well-known index funds are those that track our stock market, like the Dow Jones Industrials or the S&P 500.

Index funds are typically a much better investment than mutual funds, both because of their superior performance and because of their lower fees. Rather than trying to beat the market by selecting a small group of stocks, by investing in the market via index funds, you are beating 96 percent of the so-called experts and the mutual funds that they manage.

The main reason index funds only charge anywhere from .25 to 1 percent in annual fees is that there is no Wall Street trader in the background that gets paid trying to beat the market and other competitive funds. Fortunately the investment world is catching up to the benefits of investing in index funds over mutual funds. Index funds have recently become more than a $1 trillion market.

Getting the best deal on an index fund does require investing in the right place. Vanguard and Dimensional Funds are two such places. Vanguard's annual fees on some index funds are as low as .05 percent. Compare that to 2–3 percent annually for a mutual fund.

For those of you who may still feel that 2–3 percent does not sound like a lot, consider these fees in relation to a mutual fund's performance. A fund that appreciates 6 percent annually but charges 3 percent is taking half your earned money every year. The bottom line is that an index fund is vastly superior to a mutual fund as a compounding vehicle for your money.

Annuities

Annuities are another investment vehicle to look at for attractive compounded returns, but it does depend on what type of annuities you choose. Interestingly, annuities have something in common with our principles of wealth accumulation in that they have been around for several thousand years, with their origins reaching all the way back to the Roman Empire. Today, annuities are available from insurance companies rather than from the government as they were in Roman times.

The essence of an annuity is that money you invest will guarantee you a stream of regular payments. The longer you wait to get your first payment, the higher the payments will be. Payments are predetermined, so you will get a schedule of payments and you'll know exactly what your return will be. Annuities can also receive preferential tax treatment, allowing you to defer taxation just like with a retirement account.

Without getting into too much detail, stay away from variable annuities. They typically invest in mutual funds, and you get straddled not only by the mutual funds' excessive fees but also additional fees for the insurance company providing the annuity. All these fees can add up to almost 5 percent, which can easily eat up the majority of your earnings. This makes the tax advantages almost irrelevant since there won't be much in profits left over to defer taxes on. The only attractive feature to a variable annuity is a death-benefit guarantee. This guarantees that the beneficiaries or heirs get the entire original investment back regardless of how the underlying mutual funds perform.

A better choice is to pick a variable annuity that invests in low-cost index funds. But the best choice is a fixed indexed annuity. Many of these are tied to the S&P 500 but can be tied to other indexes or even commodities.

Fixed-index annuities combine monthly payments with low fees and outstanding guarantees regarding income and principal protection. Adding a guaranteed lifetime income rider will even guarantee you an agreed-upon minimum return regardless of market performance. Furthermore, if you combine it with a ROTH retirement account, you will receive tax-free payments for life.

As with all investments, annuities will also require research to pick the best one currently available as there are multiple options. Their increasing popularity definitely qualifies the right annuity as an investment to be considered for attractive compounded returns and preferential tax treatment.

Dividend Stocks

The average investor looks at a stock's price performance to determine whether it might be a worthwhile investment. What most people do not consider are the dividends that many stocks pay. Dividends can not only substantially boost total returns, but some dividend-paying stocks are considered by some to be the best kind of investments.

The right kind of dividend-paying stock to buy is what investment advisor Porter Stansberry wisely refers to as an *elite, dividend-paying business purchased at reasonable prices.*

A number of factors make these companies stand out. Often they are the biggest in their field with a strong competitive advantage. They also have an easily recognizable brand name, and they sell items that are considered basic necessities that will never go out of style. Examples of companies that fit these criteria are Walmart, Procter & Gamble, McDonald's, and Coca-Cola, but there are many more. Often their products are also addictive, whether it's tobacco, alcohol, sugar-filled soft drinks, fast foods, or pharmaceutical drugs. Because of this and the fact that they are mostly basic necessities, they are also recession-proof.

All of these benefits also make these elite businesses global players, where markets many times the size of the American market have yet to be fully penetrated, virtually guaranteeing substantial ongoing growth.

Total returns by companies such as these have exceeded 13 percent annually for decades. It doesn't get much better than that. Porter Stansberry provides the following example in his book *2020 America: The Survival Blueprint*. "An investment of $25,000 in a tax-deferred account that grows 13% per year for 30 years grows to nearly $1 million ($977,897)." Imagine if you started with $50,000–$100,000 or more.

The best dividend-paying companies to invest in are those with continually rising dividends. That is, their payments per share or cash distributions to investors get bigger each year. This demonstrates that these companies are not only stunningly successful at what they do, but they also care about their investors.

The dividends you receive get reinvested into additional shares making this a compounded investment. Many companies offer to make this happen automatically. It is called a dividend reinvestment plan or DRIP. Set up the DRIP with the broker you are buying your shares through and put your compounding on autopilot. It's one of the best investment moves available.

Some companies who have increased their dividends for decades, through booms and bust economies, are Walmart, Procter & Gamble, Johnson & Johnson, McDonald's, ExxonMobil, and Coca-Cola. There are more, but in the scheme of things, these companies are definitely in the minority. Nonetheless, you can find more than 200 companies that fit this criteria. Pick ones that have increased their dividend consistently each year for at least ten or twelve years. Their past performance is a strong indicator of how they will do going forward, definitely satisfying our safety requirements.

Keep in mind that the price of these companies' shares may also decline occasionally, but this provides an opportunity not to be missed. Buy their shares during a decline as this will increase the percentage dividend payout you will receive. The reason is that the dollar dividend amount will likely not go down when the price per share declines during a market fall. In fact it will probably continue to go up just like it has done year after year. This raises the percentage relationship between the dividend amount and the price of the underlying stock.

If these elite dividend-paying companies weren't already the holy grail of investing, it gets better. There is a subgroup we'll call "super elite dividend-paying companies." As you probably know, dividends are paid four times per year. But some companies occasionally make a fifth dividend payment. These are called special dividends.

Special dividends are a means of returning extra income to shareholders whenever the company has an exceptional year. They are typically not regularly recurring, but they can be quite substantial.

Finding companies that make a fifth dividend payout is not all that easy because these payouts are not reported in financial reports in the same way regularly scheduled dividends are reported. You'll have to do a little sleuthing around and solicit the help of your broker to find these companies. But once you do locate them (and if they also fit the criteria of an elite dividend-paying stock), then you've definitely found the cream of the crop.

Whole Life Insurance

This is an unusual compounded investment choice as most people don't view it as such. They view it simply as life insurance.

Companies who provide whole life insurance, as opposed to regular life insurance, are some of the safest in America. They are called mutual life insurance companies. Many of these companies are over 100 years old, and they are not traded on any stock exchange. The owners of these companies are the policy holders, not shareholders. Buy a whole life policy and you automatically become a part owner in the company. This is completely different from stock life insurance companies who have shareholders and who are not able to offer this unique product.

Mutual life insurance companies are extremely solid and pay large dividends. None have ever defaulted on their contracts in over 300 years. They are recession-proof as demand for life insurance never changes. These companies are also quite different from regular insurance companies as is the product I am describing. Because they do not report to shareholders who care only about profit, mutual life insurance companies are much more conservative and report only to their policy holders. This makes them very risk adverse and thereby one of the safest places in the world to park your money.

Whole life insurance is permanent insurance. Unlike term life insurance, whole life insurance remains in force until the policy holder dies. Whatever the amount of the policy is, that is the amount that will be paid out upon the death of the policy holder. Whole life or permanent life insurance is more like a savings plan than like traditional insurance. It also has a much higher interest rate than a regular savings account.

The return you receive from your policy, in the form of interest and dividends, is tax deferred like a retirement account because of special tax provisions established by the government. As you pay your annual premiums, you are actually able to use the money you're accumulating. This is called a policy loan. The money can be used for anything you like, without fees or penalty.

What you want to sign up for is dividend-paying whole life insurance, also known as participating whole life insurance (because you are a participant in the company's profits). Avoid all the different variations of whole life insurance that have been created in recent years. Stick to the plain vanilla version.

Because these policies are much more like savings accounts than insurance policies, you want to contribute as much as possible each year while keeping your total coverage amount as low as possible. You will earn more that way from interest and dividends. This is the opposite strategy of a regular life insurance policy where you want your payments to be as low as possible and your payout in the end as high as possible. A paid-up additions (PUA) rider enables you to do this, so ask for this rider when establishing the policy. Also discuss with your agent what your maximum annual contributions can be so that you don't cross the line and lose your tax benefits.

The dividends and interest you receive will compound for truly wealth-building results. That's what qualifies a whole life insurance policy for your consideration.

Protecting Against Declines

The average investor loses money because they have a herd mentality. When the stock market booms, they jump in, often near the peak. When the bubble bursts and the market declines, they then lose substantial amounts of money as they wait for things to turn around. Likewise when the market bottoms and everyone feels it's only going to get worse, that's when the average investor sells, only to see the market turn around shortly after and soar to new heights without his participation.

This is why contrarian investors often do very well. They do the opposite of what the masses do. They buy when stocks are cheap and sell when they see a bubble developing, when market gains become irrational. Obviously this makes all the sense in the world, but most investors do not have the know-how or discipline to invest wisely in this manner. They follow the herd, and their nest egg dies with the herd.

For this reason, once you invest, protect your investment by protecting against declines. It is a commonly known, but less commonly used, technique of setting stop-loss orders. The truth is that most people don't know when to sell a falling stock. This technique takes the guesswork out of the equation and will make big losses a thing of the past for your portfolio. In essence this is an exit strategy.

The idea is to sell your position once it has declined by a predetermined percentage of its highest valuation since you've owned it. Let's use 20 percent, but you may want to use a lower or higher percentage. If you do some research, you'll see that everyone has a different opinion on what percentage to use. Choose what feels right to you.

So let's assume you buy a stock at $100 per share. Let's further assume it rises to $200 but then starts to decline. If the high is $200, then you would sell it when it has retreated 20 percent from that high, at $160 per share. You will pocket a 60 percent return in this example.

You can place a stop-loss order with your broker, or you can discipline yourself to place the sell order when your investment retreats by 20 percent off its high. There are different theories as to which is better, but I think that with some research you'll be able to decide which is best for you.

The bottom line is that taking small losses is much better than watching your investment wither into nothingness. Executing an exit as I described, either manually or automatically, should be a mandatory part of your investment strategy. You'll be glad you did.

Consider the following compelling reason to implement this exit strategy, something very few investors realize: When you lose a certain percentage of your stock's value, the percentage needed to gain it back can be much greater. Say you own a stock at $100 per share, and it declines to $50 per share. That's a 50 percent decline. However, to get back to the original $100, it now has to double, that is, appreciate by 100 percent. That's twice the amount of the decline. In this regard the markets are stacked against you.

The following chart shows you what percentage declines have to appreciate by to get back to the original value:

Percentage Decline	Percentage appreciation required to get back to original
10%	11%
20%	25%
50%	100%
70%	333%
90%	1000%

This chart clearly shows that the farther you let your loss spiral downward, the less likely you are to get back to your original value any time soon. Therefore it makes compelling sense to keep your losses to no more than 20 or 25 percent.

***

The chapter you just read is not designed to give you investment advice as there is always additional research that should be conducted. Additionally there are frequently changes and upgrades available to the investment vehicles I describe that may not have been available at the time of writing. This chapter is designed to give you options to explore, each of which has the potential to fulfill your goal of an adequate compounded return combined with safety.

You should also remember that whatever returns you make should be reinvested if that does not happen automatically; otherwise, you will not be compounding. In the end the strength of any single investment vehicle is all in compounding, in reinvesting your income to earn more income for you. Most investments should do this automatically, but please make sure this is the case so that you don't have any surprises.

The investment options I outlined are also not the only viable options. There are certainly others, possibly even better options than what I detailed. For example, Europe is known to have stocks that pay higher dividends than American firms. I would investigate these if the dividend models appeal to you. Educate yourself and look around. With the right combination of curiosity and analysis, you will find what's best for you.

Finally, there is always the possibility of a massive and sudden restructuring of our entire system, possibly due to a major economic or currency collapse. But nothing that can happen out there can invalidate the effectiveness of the principles of wealth accumulation, whether it's compounding, leverage, or otherwise. Remember that these are timeless principles that have been around for thousands of years and will continue to be available to us regardless of economic conditions. It simply means that in the event of a major calamity that could restructure our entire financial system, we have to look elsewhere to apply the principles of wealth. In fact, we already did this. Compounding and leverage are not limited to financial instruments and real estate, for example. They can be applied in your business in a variety of ways. I provided you with several applications in the chapter titled "Applying the Secrets of Wealth."

The main lesson is in understanding and recognizing the principles of wealth accumulation. Once we are able to do that, we can apply them in a multitude of ways that may even go far beyond the examples cited in this text. You may apply them exactly as described, or you may go as far as inventing entirely new applications. Allow the understanding of these principles to occupy space in the back of your mind so that they may grant you new insight into the world around you and its potential to earn you more money than you ever thought possible.

Chapter 11:

Planning Your Approach

Planning Your Approach

As with anything, you should plan your investment approach carefully in advance. Plan your work and then work your plan. This will make a huge difference in your outcome.

Much of the information I am about to share with you in this chapter comes from my previous book *20/20 Hindsight – If I knew then what I know now I'd be a whole lot richer.* You might consider getting a copy for additional details. The book details lessons I have learned as a lifelong entrepreneur, real-life lessons you do not learn in business school. These lessons are not theory but down-in-the-trenches, invaluable street-smart lessons that will move your trajectory forward toward success as an entrepreneur in leaps and bounds.

In the book there is a chapter on goal setting called "The Only Way to Predict the Future Is to Create It." The method used here to plan your approach is essentially identical to one of the goal-setting techniques I describe in *20/20 Hindsight* called the "Baby Step Method."

Before we begin, I would like to discuss one option regarding the sequence you've seen described throughout this text. This option applies to those readers with resources beyond what most people have available to them, people who are at the very beginning stages of building their financial fortress. That option entails beginning with a leveraged investment instead of a compounded investment. Compounding, as explained previously, takes time. Leveraged investments can generate great profits in much less time, but they also often require resources not available to those people just starting out. Therefore, if you have the required resources, you can invest in a leveraged vehicle first and essentially move forward one step in our plan.

The sequence described in this text is not mandatory. It just makes the most sense for those who are new to these principles—beginners and those with limited resources. If, on the other hand, you are beyond that point, you can use the principles of wealth creation in any sequence you like, even all at once. They will still work the same. You can pick and choose, combine them, or apply only what you feel comfortable with. Each principle can make you lots of money, regardless of the order and regardless of whether you use them all or just some of them.

Wealth building does take some effort. When we look at our lives, it may sometimes seem that we have to move mountains to get from where we are to where we want to be. Making the necessary changes in our lives to achieve what we want, whatever that may be, can affect every fiber of ourselves, our families, and our lives. The task often seems massive and intimidating. Planning, research, and implementation are involved. It takes work and time. Why bother? How easy it would be to continue in the same way we always have and not attempt something that clearly looks to be more difficult than anything we're used to.

It is precisely those same destructive thoughts that have kept thousands of individuals jailed within the confines of a nine-to-five, paycheck-to-paycheck life. There is no greater temptation than to settle for less because the effort required is also less.

Not only do you have to make an effort to fulfill your goals, but you have to face the fact that it takes courage. You will be stepping into unknown territory. For those of you who take the plunge, I applaud you. You are truly deserving of the bounty that awaits you.

Because of the time it may take to reach your financial goals, your greatest challenge will be to stay on track. There are no overnight fixes. Honestly, it may take years! Even if you apply the principles of wealth in your work as well as your investments, by opening your own business for example, success will not suddenly knock on your door tomorrow morning. It takes hard work and persistence. However, it is not impossible if we know how to go about it. The secret is simple. We are not reaching for a massive change today but rather for a little change every day. And these little changes add up. Steadily, every day, we move one step closer to where we want to be.

You have everything you need for success at your disposal right now. You do not need capital to become wealthy, only the right information. You do not need luck, only hard work. In fact, the harder you work, the luckier you'll get. And you do not need a break, only persistence.

Success is not just about what you're going to get once you have it, but what you're willing to give up to get it. Are you willing to make the necessary sacrifices? Your task is not impossible, but it may not be easy either. Remember that life is not easy. Most of us think that anything difficult that confronts us is not normal, but this is blatantly false. Life is difficult. But there's a way to deal with that. Once we acknowledge that life is difficult, then suddenly it ceases being as difficult as before. Expect challenges. Expect work. Expect setbacks. They're all a part of life. Most of all, accept change. Ironically, change is the only permanent thing we have. Once you accept all these things, even welcome them as learning and growing experiences, watch your life transform. Watch the level of control that you exert over your life's direction increase dramatically.

There is a way to deal with major tasks, such as implementing all the strategies and principles outlined in this book, and that is by breaking them down into manageable steps. Consider this: the great pyramids of Egypt were not built overnight, nor did their makers claim the task would be too daunting. Knowing that the pyramids would take generations to build, the builders went ahead with the task anyway. Ultimately the pyramids were completed, and now we refer to them as one of the seven man-made wonders of the world. What did they know that we don't?

Think about this: What if you were given the same assignment, to build a pyramid that would rival those built by the ancients? Most people would give up without ever starting. Too many bricks, not enough hours in the day, or lack of strength are a few of the endless rationalizations you could invent. After all, we have all had a lifetime to perfect our personal techniques of rationalization.

But what if you placed one brick at a time, just one brick every day, into a large field near your home, day after day, without fail. Eventually you will have built a pyramid worthy of an appearance in your local newspaper, maybe even in the *Guinness World Records*. By breaking down the job that at first seemed impossible into many small steps or objectives, you have suddenly eliminated all chances of failure. Your pyramid will grow, brick by brick, until completion. It's that simple.

Always remember, monumental achievements are nothing more than the accumulation of many small, achievable efforts. Failures come from those individuals who give up or don't even start.

In the same fashion, the vast majority of individuals fail at goal-setting techniques, not because their goals are too optimistic but because the steps are too large. To illustrate, do not set yourself the goal of earning $10,000 all at once but rather earning the same amount in $100 increments, one after another. Either way, the end result is the same, and guess which path is easier.

After reading this book, you should go back over everything once more, and you should start by setting goals for yourself first. They should be optimistic yet realistic. You must describe, in writing, exactly where you want to be and when you want to be there. Then you can create a path to get there using the method I will outline for you shortly.

The best book I have found dedicated to goal setting is *The Path of Least Resistance* by Robert Fritz. Fritz shatters our belief that, if outer circumstances are changed, inner changes also result. The opposite is true. If we learn to make certain changes in our thoughts—that is, by making inner changes—these result in predictable external changes. His methods are not wishful thinking; they truly work.

What Fritz teaches us to change are the fundamental underlying structures of our lives. These are analogous to a riverbed. If we change the path of a riverbed, not through force but rather by a gentle reconstruction of the riverbed itself (our thoughts), the flow of water automatically changes direction (our external environment). Our thoughts are our fundamental underlying structures. If we alter these, our external world will automatically change also, following the path of least resistance just as water would.

The thoughts that I want you to change have to do with your self-imposed limitations, believing there is something, anything, that you cannot do. Wrong! You can do it. You can build a successful business if you want one. You can make the principles in this book work for you. You can become rich. Yes, you can. You have everything you need at your disposal already. You just need to use those resources. Willingness and a desire to learn what you don't know are at the top of that list.

In regards to this text, your first step is to decide where you want to end up financially. This is the same as creating a goal. Do you want to be a multimillionaire within ten years? Decide what you want and when you want it and then write it down. Don't be shy about setting yourself an ambitious goal as I will show you how to fulfill it. Do what I did a long time ago. I took the word "impossible" out of my vocabulary. Do the same. Trust me—you'll be glad you did.

You need to have a clear goal in mind for a very specific reason. Basil S. Walsh said it best. "If you don't know where you are going, how can you expect to get there?" Have a vision and a goal. Plan your work and then work your plan.

Your next step is to use the baby-step goal-setting technique to create a predetermined path from A to B. Here's how.

Write your financial goal at the top of a piece of paper and describe your current financial situation at the very bottom. Be very detailed and be honest about where you are right now. Don't sugarcoat it and don't sell yourself short either. Just be realistic.

The middle of the page will be filled in with a path. First, create major steps, such as the principles outlined in this book. For example, above your current reality at the bottom, write your first major step, saving 10 percent of your income. The next major step above that one, one step closer to your goal at the top, might be investing those savings in a compounded investment. Above that might be a leveraged investment, and so on.

Once you have created a ladder of major steps that will take you from where you are to where you want to be, you will provide the detail. By "detail" I mean you need to break down the major steps into several small steps. I call these baby steps because they need to be small enough so that each is ridiculously easy to achieve, just like placing one brick a day to build a pyramid.

Your first major step of saving 10 percent should have several baby steps right below it taking you there. These could include opening a separate savings account to hold your saved funds, segregated from any other accounts you may have. Another baby step might involve the exact mechanics you will follow to deduct your 10 percent from every paycheck or source of income before anything else gets paid. You decide.

Between saving 10 percent and investing those funds into a compounded investment, you will also insert baby steps. One of these should definitely be researching which compounded vehicle you will choose. Another might be involving a broker to help you, reading additional books on the subject, etc. Then do the same process for your leveraged investment above your compounding investment. The principles in this text can provide you with the major steps. You will choose the order that is appropriate for your situation, such as choosing which comes first, leverage or compounding. Then you'll insert multiple baby steps. Remember that your baby steps have to be small and easily achievable by anyone. That's the secret, taking a big goal and breaking it down into numerous tiny steps until the act of sequentially fulfilling each tiny step will eventually get you to a goal that otherwise would have seemed out of reach.

All you are doing is breaking a big goal down into many small achievable steps and creating a road map from A to B. Follow the map and you'll get there. The following is an example of what it might look like. Everyone's will look a bit different. The sequence may vary, as may the number of steps:

Description of Financial Goal (include a deadline)
⇧
Major Step #5 (with deadline)
⇧
Baby Step
⇧
Baby Step
⇧
Baby Step
⇧
Major Step #4 (with deadline)
⇧
Baby Step
⇧
Baby Step
⇧
Baby Step
⇧
Major Step #3 (with deadline)
⇧
Baby Step
⇧
Baby Step
⇧
Baby Step
⇧
Major Step #2 (with deadline)
⇧
Baby Step
⇧
Baby Step
⇧
Baby Step
⇧
Major Step#1 (with deadline)
⇧
Baby Step
⇧
Baby Step
⇧
Baby Step
⇧
Description of Current Financial Situation (include today's date)

Your path will take you from bottom to top. Obviously, the number of major steps and the number of baby steps will vary from person to person as everyone will have a different plan. The point is that whatever your path, the baby-step method is a predetermined path, taking you along a known route of small achievable steps. Nothing is left to chance. All you need to do is move from one baby step to the next, and eventually you'll get to the top. You can use this method for achieving any goal where the path from where you are to where you want to be can be mapped.

Here is a synopsis of the major steps discussed so far. As mentioned, you may adjust the order according to your situation.

1) Acquire the right knowledge.

2) Describe your goals.

3) Plan your work using the baby-step method.

4) Save at least 10 percent of your income.*

5) Invest your savings.

6) Compound your earnings.*

7) Leverage your money.*

8) Continue saving.

9) Create risk capital (income from savings plan).

10)Invest for more than you borrow (100% leverage).*

*Key financial principle

Up until now we have been building a recipe for success. But what about failure? Isn't it unrealistic to assume that we may never fail? Yes, but it is how we view failure and how we deal with it that will eventually determine who succeeds and who stays behind in a mediocre lifestyle.

Telephone salespeople deal with rejection at least nine out of ten times they pick up the phone. The smart salesperson knows, however, that with every failure he or she is one step closer to succeeding. Every successful person has had failures, but they kept going. Many millionaires have gone broke two or three times before acquiring lasting wealth. There are more lessons to be learned from your failures than from your successes. Failure is opportunity in every case.

True character is revealed when one comes face-to-face with adversity. Yet an even more humbling experience can come from success itself as it is often the cause for failure. Few know how to guard against this trap until they learn the hard way. You see, success breeds complacency, the breeding ground for financial mistakes. Anyone who has had instant financial success in business, for example, knows this because they have probably lost it all since their first success. Maybe they forgot to keep an eye on the competition, ignored cost-controlling measures, or simply forgot to maintain a smooth-running financial enterprise. All are the result of complacency. With this foreknowledge and some self-discipline, you will hopefully be able to avoid this trap.

On a grand scale, the Reagan era provides a stunning example of how success can breed failure. When Ronald Reagan was elected to office, he had a vision and a plan. His vision was to revitalize the American economy and military. His plan was to cut taxes and implement the theories described by John Maynard Keynes.

Keynesian economics dictated that to stimulate an economy, you have to inject huge amounts of capital. Printing money would lead to inflation, so you borrow the capital instead (the principle of leverage). By going into debt, America experienced the greatest economic boom the world had ever seen. Employment and tax receipts soared. Everybody benefited, rich and poor alike. Trickledown economics worked, regardless of what some people would like you to believe.

Reagan's popularity ratings went through the roof as America was poised to alter the Constitution so that we could elect Reagan to a third term. However, the success of Reagan's policies also became their demise. Reagan became complacent as he rode a wave of popularity and prosperity. He neglected to implement the second half of Keynes' formula: once you have borrowed your way to prosperity, you then use the financial machine you have created to pay back your debt. Reagan never took this step during his second term, partly due to a reluctant mega-spending Congress, and ever-increasing debt resulted, debt that continues to this day. Granted, the debt created by Reagan was a pittance compared to the mountainous disaster we are facing today.

So how important is it for us to plan for tomorrow. To quote an individual very close to me, "I would rather live it up today than worry about tomorrow." How sad. There's a lot to be said for *Carpe diem*, "Seize the day," but we still have to plan for tomorrow. Tomorrow will come, and it will come sooner than we care to admit.

Remember how careless you were as a teenager thinking that adulthood was an eternity away? You thought it would never come. So did I. So did every other person on the planet. But it did come. Responsibilities and the need to earn a living appeared from out of nowhere. Whatever our age, time will not slow down for us, nor will we be given another chance. We must seize the opportunity NOW.

The future, whether we plan for it or not, will arrive. Not surprisingly, if we plan for it, the quality of our lives will improve along the way. Peace of mind, hope, and most importantly, a sense of purpose will be our ultimate reward.

Having a sense of purpose in our lives is essential to our survival. It is rivaled only by our need for air, food, and water. Without purpose we ultimately expire. Just look at the many seniors who retire at age sixty-five in good health only to pass away at age sixty-six. If purpose is taken out of a productive life, the individual is literally left to die of boredom. An empty shell always withers until it eventually collapses. Your future, a better future for you and your family, should be your purpose.

Work for its own sake can be the reward, at least part of it. It provides us with purpose. Even if the monetary profit is not always high, there is a higher motive. Consider a multimillion-dollar company opening a supermarket chain. Grocery stores typically operate on a 1–3 percent profit margin. The corporation could do a whole lot better by investing their money in a CD earning 6 percent or more. Obviously, return on investment wasn't the only consideration. Compensation can come in many forms. It is the same with us. We work for the sake of working (for the sense of purpose it gives us), besides working for profit.

The quest for wealth, if there is a positive motive for it, is a worthy goal providing purpose to young and old alike. Best of all we can provide ourselves with this gem. We do not have to wait for someone to tell us what to do or when to do it. Nor can someone tell us to retire from our quest. Unfortunately, we live in a society where the odds of achieving financial prosperity are stacked against us, but it can be done. Getting rich is about beating the system. Whether creating wealth is merely a game to you or living well is your personal revenge, you can win if you learn the rules of success.

The only limitations that can keep you from your dreams are your own self-imposed limitations. According to Mary Kay Ash, if you believe you can, you probably can. If you believe you can't, you probably can't. The only difference between yourself and one of the thousands of self-made millionaires in this country is self-imposed limitations. They believed they could do it.

As a final word of advice, you must recognize that the only place where success comes before work is in the dictionary. If you are new to the concept of effort, your first obligation will be to sacrifice your false sense of comfort. People who believe life without sacrifice or problems is even remotely possible are living in a state of illusion. Life is difficult. Recognize this simple truism and life will eventually cease to be difficult.

It is within the difficulties of our lives that we may also find opportunity. In China the symbol for crisis is the same as the one for opportunity. We must recognize and seize opportunities when they present themselves. The old proverb "opportunity only knocks once" is often frighteningly true. But a different opportunity will always present itself. If not, don't wait for it to knock. You knock—hard. Create your own opportunity. Nonetheless, keep your eyes open because there is opportunity in your town, wherever you may be, waiting to be discovered. Interestingly, the more opportunities you recognize and seize, the more that will reveal themselves to you. This novel quirk is just another example of the multiplier effect we have discovered in several discussions throughout this text. In other words, it is an abstract application of the principle of compounding.

In the well-known essay by Russel Conwell entitled "Acres of Diamonds," we are told about an ancient Persian named Ali Hafed. It was said that Ali Hafed owned a very large farm. He was wealthy and content. He was content because he was wealthy, wealthy because he was content. One day a vagabond Buddhist priest told him all about diamonds. He told him what they are worth, how nature created them, and how much power they bestow upon their owner.

That night Ali Hafed went to bed a poor man. He was poor because he was discontented, and he was discontented because he feared he was poor because he didn't own any diamonds.

Soon thereafter Ali set out to find diamonds. He sold his house and his land to commence a trek that led him through Palestine and, years later, all the way into Europe. In old age he reached Barcelona where, still without having found diamonds, he desperately cast himself into the surf between the Pillars of Hercules. His final breath was one of resignation and despair.

Meanwhile, the man who purchased Ali Hafed's farm one day noticed a flash of light, bright as sunshine, from the sand in his stream. He brought home the brightly colored stone and showed it to the same Buddhist priest who, years earlier, had taught Ali Hafed all about diamonds. The priest immediately recognized the telltale sparkle of a lustrous diamond. This stone was the first diamond found in what was to become the diamond mine of Galconda. It eventually produced not only the Kohinoor but also the largest of the English and Russian crown jewels. Had Ali Hafed remained at home to dig in his wheat fields he would have had "acres of diamonds."

Examine your assets, your hobbies, your abilities, and your knowledge. Opportunity can be found everywhere. Then start your journey today.

If you arm yourself with the mindset that making some minor sacrifices along the way is absolutely inevitable—if you want to fulfill your dreams—you will never be disappointed or intimidated when an occasional obstacle needs to be overcome. Each obstacle presents an opportunity. Seize it. You will truly reap the benefits of what you sow.

Procrastination is the easiest trap for us to fall into. It is the art of postponing work indefinitely. There is no greater evil than inaction. It is addicting. It seems to feed on itself and make us lazier with every postponement of action. Once we start procrastinating, we will do it again and again. It is, however, comforting to know that when we do take that first step, the same multiplier effect will progressively increase our motivation, thus making the next steps easier. That is, we build up momentum.

Often procrastination is the result of rationalization: "Why do now what I can put off until tomorrow?" We also tend to peg our efforts to specific events: "I will start on New Year's Day and make it my New Year's resolution." Sound familiar? Stop fooling yourself. If you want to make a change, make it now. There's only one way to get something done and that is to do it. And there is just one guaranteed road to success. Never, never, never give up.

Press On

"Nothing in the world can take the place of persistence.

Talent will not; nothing is more common than

unsuccessful men with talent.

Genius will not; unrewarded genius is almost a proverb.

Education alone will not; the world is full of

educated derelicts. Persistence and determination

alone are omnipotent."

–Calvin Coolidge

About the Author

---•●•---

For 25 years, Parviz Firouzgar has been the owner of numerous multi-million dollar companies in a variety of industries, sometimes running several ventures simultaneously, both for profit and nonprofit entities. Some of Parviz's companies involved the use of investor funds of up to several million dollars. As mentioned, one investor walked away with $1.7 million in one year as a result of his confidence in the author's abilities when Parviz was just in his 20's.

Parviz founded a mortgage company and employed over 500 loan officers. He wrote business plans for startup companies that helped them raise many millions in startup capital. After he discovered a new way of raising funds, he expanded into the charitable arena. Within one year, his company was supporting 2,300 needy children around the world, providing all their food, clothing, and education.

Parviz has been in the direct mail and sweepstakes business, mailing so many millions of pieces of mail each month that his local post office had to expand their operations. Most recently, he has been in the precious metals and diamond business, including owning a gold mine.

Parviz was a radio talk show host and a long time instructor for Income Builders International (IBI), now called CEO Space, an entrepreneurial forum with internationally recognized instructors, such as: Jack Canfield, Mark Victor Hansen, Bob Proctor, T. Harv Eker, John Gray, and Lisa Nichols.

Raised in Europe, Parviz speaks four languages. He has been accepted for membership in Mensa and Intertel, both high I.Q. societies.

Acknowledgements

---•◆•---

I would like to thank my publisher Robbin Simons of Crescendo Publishing, LLC for being such an outstanding and reliable businesswoman. She does business the way everyone should, on schedule. Thank you also to my cover and web designer Melodye Hunter, my editor Sharon Honeycutt, project manager Kate Lemberg, and interior layout and design guru Zonoiko Arafat. I have really enjoyed taking this journey with such an outstanding team and I look forward to us all working together again on my next book.

Connect with Parviz Firouzgar

Facebook: www.facebook.com/pfirouzgar

LinkedIn: www.linkedin.com/pub/parviz-firouzgar/b6/8b4/91

Twitter: @ParvizFirouzgar

Website: www.ParvizFirouzgar.com

Email: Parviz@ParvizFirouzgar.com

In Gratitude to You

I would be so grateful if you could take a minute or two to share what you loved about this book and provide an honest review on our Amazon sales page.